POPULAR DAY HIKES

The Castle and Crowsnest

POPULAR DAY HIKES

The Castle and Crowsnest

ANDREW NUGARA

RMB

For information on purchasing bulk quantities of this book, or to obtain media excerpts or invite the author to speak at an event, please visit rmbooks.com and select the "Contact" tab.

RMB | Rocky Mountain Books Ltd.
rmbooks.com
@rmbooks
facebook.com/rmbooks

Cataloguing data available from Library and Archives Canada
ISBN 9781771605137 (paperback)
ISBN 9781771605144 (electronic)

All photographs are by Andrew Nugara unless otherwise noted.

Interior design by Colin Parks
Cover photo by Matthew Clay.

Printed and bound in Canada

We would like to also take this opportunity to acknowledge the traditional territories upon which we live and work. In Calgary, Alberta, we acknowledge the Niitsítapi (Blackfoot) and the people of the Treaty 7 region in Southern Alberta, which includes the Siksika, the Piikuni, the Kainai, the Tsuut'ina and the Stoney Nakoda First Nations, including Chiniki, Bearpaw, and Wesley First Nations. The City of Calgary is also home to Métis Nation of Alberta, Region III. In Victoria, British Columbia, we acknowledge the traditional territories of the Lkwungen (Esquimalt, and Songhees), Malahat, Pacheedaht, Scia'new, T'Sou-ke and W̱SÁNEĆ (Pauquachin, Tsartlip, Tsawout, Tseycum) peoples.

We acknowledge the financial support of the Government of Canada through the Canada Book Fund and the Canada Council for the Arts, and of the province of British Columbia through the British Columbia Arts Council and the Book Publishing Tax Credit.

Disclaimer
The actions described in this book may be considered inherently dangerous activities. Individuals undertake these activities at their own risk. The information put forth in this guide has been collected from a variety of sources and is not guaranteed to be completely accurate or reliable. Many conditions and some information may change owing to weather and numerous other factors beyond the control of the authors and publishers. Individuals or groups must determine the risks, use their own judgment, and take full responsibility for their actions. Do not depend on any information found in this book for your own personal safety. Your safety depends on your own good judgment based on your skills, education, and experience.

It is up to the users of this guidebook to acquire the necessary skills for safe experiences and to exercise caution in potentially hazardous areas. The authors and publishers of this guide accept no responsibility for your actions or the results that occur from another's actions, choices, or judgments. If you have any doubt as to your safety or your ability to attempt anything described in this guidebook, do not attempt it.

Contents

Area Maps

The Castle East

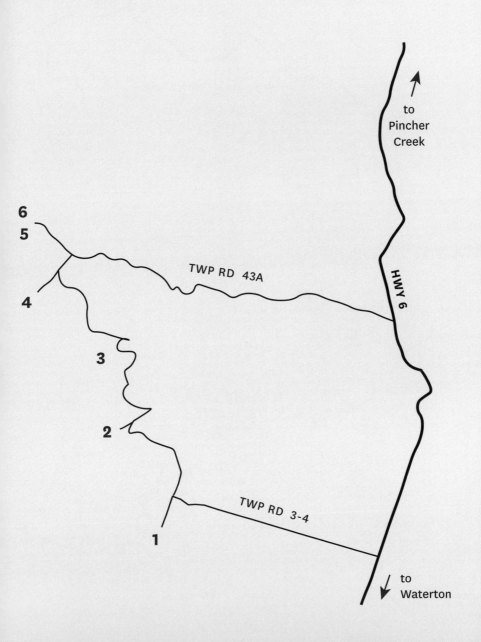

The Castle West

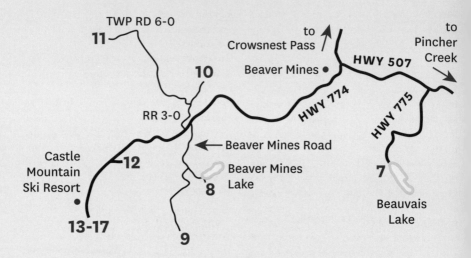

11 — TWP RD 6-0

10

RR 3-0

to Crowsnest Pass

Beaver Mines • HWY 507

to Pincher Creek

HWY 774

HWY 775

Beaver Mines Road ←

Castle Mountain Ski Resort •

12

8 Beaver Mines Lake

7 Beauvais Lake

13-17

9

Crowsnest

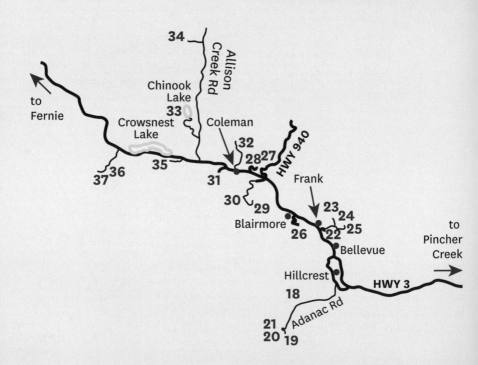

34

Allison Creek Rd

Chinook Lake

33

to Fernie

Crowsnest Lake

Coleman

32

28 27

HWY 940

Frank

37 36

35

31

30

29

Blairmore

26

23

24 25

22

Bellevue

Hillcrest

18

Adanac Rd

to Pincher Creek

HWY 3

21

20 19

Introduction

About Castle Provincial Park and Castle Wildland Provincial Park

Castle Provincial Park and Castle Wildland Provincial Park sit immediately north of southern Alberta's stunning Waterton Lakes National Park. The two parks combined presently encompass 1050 square kilometres of land. In comparison, Waterton Lakes National Park is 505 square kilometres and Banff National Park is 6641 square kilometres. The Castle area has quite recently (2017) gained the status of a provincial park and therefore is now afforded a welcome measure of environmental protection. Note that in this guidebook, for the sake of simplicity, Castle Provincial Park and Castle Wildland Provincial Park are used interchangeably, as they encompass one large and contiguous area; the term "The Castle" is often used to describe the entire area.

Like Waterton, for many, The Castle's primary attraction is the colourful rock, far-reaching views and stunning lakes. Although an excellent system of trails has been developed throughout the park, The Castle still enjoys a remote and wild feeling. Those choosing to leave the beaten path and seek a mountain summit will likely have that mountain all to themselves.

Pincher Creek is the closest town to The Castle. There you can find all amenities, including food, hotels and motels. Numerous campgrounds throughout the park allow for more rustic accommodation.

About Crowsnest

Crowsnest Pass lies northwest of Castle Provincial Park. At present (2020) the Crowsnest has the singular distinction of being the only area in the Canadian Rockies from Waterton to Jasper that does not have a park or reserve designation. This is primarily due to the area's historical significance as a coal mining community and therefore home to many private mining companies. Privatization of land in the Crowsnest still occurs. It is up to the hiker to be cognizant of private lands and stay off them, even if they used to be public. Also note that signage can change or be noticeably lacking for some hikes.

The topography and geology of the Crowsnest area are strikingly different from its southeasterly neighbour. The colourful argillites, shales and dolostones of The Castle are replaced with relatively uniform grey limestone. Mountains in the Crowsnest tend to stand in relative isolation from one another, and although there are groups of peaks connected by ridges, very few of those ridges are traversable. Note that some of the far northwest end of the Crowsnest area is now a part of Castle Wildland Provincial Park. However, again for the sake of simplicity, trips in that area are described in the Crowsnest section, as they are accessed through Crowsnest Pass.

Crowsnest is also home to several geological marvels: Turtle Mountain, Crowsnest Mountain and The Promised Land. These destinations are not to be missed by hikers and scramblers looking for an adventurous and challenging day out. Note that Crowsnest Mountain is not included in this book. It is a serious scramble that should not be taken lightly. Refer to Alan Kane's *Scrambles in the Canadian Rockies, 3rd Edition* for details.

Crowsnest Pass is comprised of five communities: Hillcrest, Bellevue, Frank, Blairmore and Coleman.

Getting there

For The Castle see Area Maps 1 and 2 on pages 5 and 6. Both areas of The Castle are accessed from Pincher Creek: Highway 6 south gets you to the east section of the park, while Highways 507 and 774 go to the west section.

For Crowsnest Pass see Area Map 3, also at page 6. Highway 3 provides access to all areas of Crowsnest Pass.

The Castle and Crowsnest are both about 2.5–3 hours from Calgary and 1.5 hours from Lethbridge. Car is the best mode of transportation to get to either destination. Note that neither area presently (2021) requires a park pass.

Facilities

Pincher Creek provides the bulk of amenities for The Castle, offering a variety of hotels and motels. There are many restaurants, from casual to fine dining. At present The Castle does not have a visitor centre, but information is available by calling 403-627-1165 or toll free from anywhere in Alberta by dialling 310-0000 followed by the 10-digit phone number.

Amenities can be found in all five communities of Crowsnest Pass, although Coleman and Blairmore are the most significantly developed.

Weather

In general, the summer months in The Castle and Crowsnest are beautifully sunny and very warm (up to the mid-30s). However, both areas are subject to very high winds. Check the forecast, with special attention to wind speeds, before you plan a trip.

The fall can be exceptionally pleasant, with more moderate temperatures, and extended periods of stable weather. The larches change colour in the latter part of September and first part of October, making it an ideal time to visit The Castle (larches are less common in Crowsnest).

Hiking opportunities are limited during the winter, as both areas usually get a significant amount of snow. Ski touring and snowshoeing are great ways to explore The Castle and Crowsnest from December to May.

Drinking-water

To be safe, it is best to bring your own water or that from hotels, campgrounds etc. Natural sources may be contaminated with *Giardia lamblia*, a parasite that can cause severe gastrointestinal problems. At higher elevations it is generally safer to drink from streams without treating the water. Filtering the water is also an option.

Wildlife concerns

Wildlife is abundant in The Castle and Crowsnest. Deer, elk, moose, bears and many others make their homes here and have more right to the land than humans do. Stay away the animals and DO NOT feed any form of wildlife. When hiking, make lots of noise to warn bears and other wildlife of your presence. Moose and elk can be aggressive in the fall, during mating season — steer well clear if you encounter them.

Unfortunately the other form of wildlife prevalent in The Castle and Crowsnest is ticks. From March to the end of June ticks ravenously feed on any mammal they can sink their mouthparts into, humans included. Check yourself carefully after any early season hike.

Safety tips

- If you are hiking alone, let someone know where you are going. Make lots of noise while you are hiking. Most bear attacks involve solo hikers.
- Don't be lulled into a false sense of security because you are in a larger group. You still must make noise to warn bears and other wildlife of your presence.
- Carry bear spray and know how to use it.
- Consider using a personal locator device, such as SPOT, in case of an emergency.
- Stay on designated trails unless you are experienced and/or familiar with the challenges of off-trail hiking/scrambling.
- Check the weather forecast in advance. Also, check the internet and the visitor centre for trail conditions and trail and area closures.

- Afternoon thunderstorms are common in the summer. Start early to avoid them.

Campgrounds

THE CASTLE:

- Beauvais Lake. Call 403-627-1165 or reserve online through Alberta Parks Reservation, reserve.albertaparks.ca.
- Beaver Mines Lake. Call 403-627-1165.
- Castle Falls. Call 403-627-1165.
- Castle River Bridge. Call 403-627-1165.
- Lynx Creek. Call 403-627-1165.
- Southfork Lakes. Primitive backcountry campground.
- Middlepass Lakes (BC). Primitive backcountry campground.
- Bovin Lake. Primitive backcountry campground.

CROWSNEST:

- Lundbreck Falls. Call 403-627-1165.
- Chinook Lake. Call 403-627-1165.
- Crowsnest Pass. Call 403-564-4814

Using this book

HOW THE TRAILS WERE CHOSEN

As a relatively new provincial park, The Castle is home only to a small number of hiking trails. Therefore, almost all of The Castle trails are represented in this book. Only the trails that have few redeeming features or are extremely remote with access challenges have been left out.

Crowsnest Pass has many more trails than The Castle. The routes were chosen according to popularity and from talking to other guidebook authors. A special thanks to Joey Ambrosi and Dave McMurray for their invaluable contributions and advice in this regard.

TRAILS

Trail development, signage and maintenance for The Castle is in a state of flux. Given The Castle's relatively new designation as a provincial park, Alberta Parks is in the process of developing and signing new trails. As such, expect changes in the future to information found in this book. In addition, some trails, specifically The Castle East, are accessed via gas roads and sometimes devoid of signage. Having said that, the overwhelming majority of the trails are well-established and easy to follow.

Most of the trails in Crowsnest have been long established. They are well worn and therefore easy to follow. However, because the area is not a provincial or national park, trail signage in Crowsnest is noticeably lacking.

OPTIONS

Text in other colours indicates an option to extend the trip and/or make a side trip: Going farther...

DISTANCES

Distances represent the round-trip distance for each trip.

HEIGHT GAIN

Height gains represent the total height gain for each round trip, including any significant ups and downs along the way.

HIGH POINT

Included only for those trips that require a moderate to significant height gain and/or reach a summit.

RATING

The ratings used in this book are Very easy, Easy, Moderate and Strenuous. Qualifiers have been included with trips rated Strenuous. That is, strenuous based on length or on steepness or on both length and steepness.

SEASON

This recommends which time of the year to do the trip. Note that late spring and/or early autumn snow can dramatically affect the length of the hiking season from year to year.

DIFFICULTY

Describes conditions underfoot and the steepness of the grades. It is assumed that the trips are undertaken with good hiking conditions, but adverse weather or snowy conditions may elevate the rating.

Scrambling sections in this book are generally defined as very steep hiking, often without a trail, and/or ascending small rock steps, requiring use of the hands.

SKETCH MAPS

Solid red lines indicate main trails. Dashed red lines indicate optional routes and/or Going farther routes.

DO I NEED ANY OTHER MAPS?

For all hikes in The Castle use NTS (National Topographic System) maps 82 G/01 Sage Creek and G/08 Beaver Mines. For the Crowsnest area use G/09 Blairmore, G/10 Crowsnest and G/15 Tornado Mountain.

If you are using technology, getting the *Topo Maps Canada* app on your phone is ideal. The app uses a satellite signal, not a cellphone signal, to pinpoint your exact location and then shows that location on a topographical map. Therefore, you can be far out of cellphone range but still determine your location. The maps on the app also show many of the trails in The Castle and Crowsnest.

WHAT TO WEAR

Hiking boots, as opposed to runners, are highly recommended for all the trails. If you are going off-trail for some of the more scrambly terrain, then a good pair of sturdy boots is essential. Bring a rain jacket and warm clothes, as the weather can change dramatically and very quickly. For those hot summer days, bring sunscreen, a hat and bug-repellent.

Doing more

For more hiking opportunities similar to those in The Castle and Crowsnest, drive south into Waterton National Park (note that the Kenow fire of 2017 damaged much of this park and trail access may be limited). Alternatively, grab your passport and head even farther south, across the border and into the jewel of Montana, Glacier National Park. The system of trails in this park is staggering and hiking them will keep you occupied and mesmerized for years. In Canada, Kananaskis Country, Banff, Lake Louise, Yoho, Jasper and many other areas offer the same quality of world-class hiking that is commonplace in The Castle and Crowsnest. Check out other books in the Popular Day Hikes series, specifically *Popular Day Hikes: Kananaskis Country — Revised & Updated*, by Gillean Daffern, and *Popular Day Hikes: Canadian Rockies — Revised & Updated*, by Tony Daffern, both from 2019.

The logical extension of hiking is scrambling — getting to the top of a mountain without technical means (i.e., ropes and climbing equipment). Acquire copies of Alan Kane's *Scrambles in the Canadian Rockies, 3rd Edition* and my own *More Scrambles in the Canadian Rockies, 3rd Edition* for detailed information and route descriptions.

THE TRAILS

CASTLE
PROVINCIAL
PARK

For the purposes of this book, trips in The Castle have been divided into two sections: The Castle East (all trips accessed from Highway 6 south of Pincher Creek) and The Castle West (all trips accessed from Highways 507 and 774 west of Pincher Creek).

◄ *Looking down the Yarrow Creek valley from near the summit of Spionkop Ridge.*

THE CASTLE EAST

Colours of The Castle, on Loaf Mountain.

1 Yarrow Creek

A serious workout in beautiful surroundings. Easy hiking, but lots of it!

DISTANCE 26 km return
HEIGHT GAIN 550 m
HIGH POINT 2005 m
STRENUOUS length
SUMMER, EARLY FALL

Start: From the south end of Pincher Creek, drive 30.6 km south on Highway 6 and turn right onto Spread Eagle Road (TWP RD 3-4, 4.2 km south of the general store in Twin Butte). Drive 8 km to the end of the road, turn left onto Yarrow Creek Road (RGE RD 30-3) and go 1.2 km to the end of that road, where the trailhead lies. Note that the first part of the nearby gas road goes through private property and is NOT an option for hikers.

Difficulty: Muddy, sometimes sloppy trail at the beginning, then gravel road, then a hard-packed trail to the lake. The latter half of the gravel gas road and some of the trail is bikeable, but getting your bike to the gravel road has its challenges and is not worth the effort.

1. Hike south on the obvious trail. Early in the season or after rain, this trail can be a sloppy mess for short sections. Go through a gate and continue on the wide trail.

2. When the trail eventually descends towards Yarrow Creek, either make your way directly onto the gravel gas road by crossing Yarrow Creek or stay on the north side of the creek and follow it to the bridge that goes over the creek. Join up with the gas road here.

3. Hike west to the end of the gas road, staying on the north side of the creek.

4. At the far end of the gas road, find the Yarrow Creek trail, down near the left side. Follow the trail for approximately 6.5 km to an unnamed tarn. Ignore the trails that branch off to the left. Views of lengthy Spionkop Ridge on the right improve throughout.

5. Hike around the tarn if desired. A trail continues past the lake to a couple of scenic waterfalls (sometimes reduced to large drips by late summer!)

6. Return the same way you came in or consider making it a REALLY long day by continuing up to Spionkop Ridge and/or Newman Peak

▲ One of the few opportunities to go right down to Yarrow Creek, with Spionkop Ridge in the background.

▼ The west end of the tarn.

▲ *Typical terrain from near the col. The ascent ridge is on the left and is much easier than it looks.*

▼ *The million-dollar view from Spionkop Ridge. Perhaps the best viewpoint in The Castle.*
PHOTO MATTHEW CLAY.

Going farther to the summit of Spionkop Ridge

Hike and scramble up to a surreal viewpoint, featuring a magnificent view of Spionkop Ridge, Loaf Mountain and many others.

> DISTANCE add 4.8 km return
> HEIGHT GAIN add 540 m
> HIGH POINT 2576 m
> VERY STRENUOUS steepness and length

1. There is a track leading up the mountainside, starting from the east end of the trail. However, it is preferable (more scenic) to continue on the main trail, past the lake and up to the headwall, where you might find a few cascades of water coming down the rock.

2. At the headwall, turn right and head up steeper terrain, picking the line of least resistance up the mountain.

3. A short distance up, trend to the left, directly up towards the summit, intercepting a good trail going left and up the mountain. Follow that trail and then make your way, via scree slopes and animal trails, to the low col (C) south of the summit (S) (see photo on opposite page).

4. From the col, turn north and scramble easily to the summit. Enjoy the wonderful view and then return the same way you came in. More-direct routes down to the lake are possible if you are comfortable on steeper terrain.

◄ *From just past the tarn, the route to the col (C) is visible, as is the summit (S).*

Going farther to the summit of Newman Peak

Newman Peak is more commonly ascended from the Waterton side, via Goat Lake. However, if you have outrageous amounts of energy and knee cartilage, the summit can be reached from Spionkop. Expect a few short sections of moderate scrambling.

> **DISTANCE** add 4 km return from Spionkop Ridge
> **HEIGHT GAIN** add 150 m
> **HIGH POINT** 2515 m
> **VERY STRENUOUS** steepness and length

1. Descend south to the col between the two peaks.

2. Continue up the other side, circumventing more difficult terrain by swinging out to the right if necessary. Return the same way you came in. Unless there is a helicopter with the keys left in it sitting at the summit of either, resist the urge to continue on to "Newman Senior" or Avion Ridge!

▼ *Newman Peak (centre), as seen from near the col. "Newman Senior" is to the left, Avion Ridge to the right.*

▼▼ *An early season view to the west from Newman Peak.*

2 Spionkop Creek

A wonderful, long hike between Spionkop Ridge and Loaf Mountain. Reaching the summits of either or both of these statuesque peaks is also an option. Biking the approach is recommended.

DISTANCE 18 km return

HEIGHT GAIN 720 m

HIGH POINT 2280 m

STRENUOUS length

SUMMER, EARLY FALL

Start: From the south end of Pincher Creek, 30.6 km south on Highway 6 and turn right onto Spread Eagle Road (TWP RD 3-4, 4.2 km south of the general store in Twin Butte). Go 8 km to a T-junction and turn right onto Yarrow Creek Road (RGE RD 30-3). After 4 km, having crossed Spionkop Creek bridge, take a hairpin turn and then the first left to the locked gate. Park on the side of the road and do not block the gate.

Difficulty: 4 km of wide gravel road, followed by 5 km of good trail but potentially overgrown in places. Off-trail for Loaf and Spionkop.

1. Hike (or, preferably, bike) the gas road for 4 km to its end.

2. The road is replaced by a good trail that goes most of the way up the valley. The first 2.3 km of this trail, to where the trail forks, are relatively easy to bike. Leave your bike here and take the right-hand fork.

3. The trail gains elevation and continues up the increasingly scenic valley, with Loaf Mountain on the right side and Spionkop Ridge on the left.

4. Stay to the right at the next fork as you get closer to the base of Loaf Mountain. The trail eventually goes into the forest and can be overgrown but is still easy to follow.

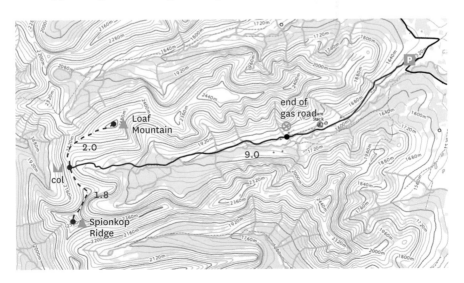

▲ At the end of the gas road. The trail goes into the trees at the right. Don't expect the deer to be there!

▼ The outrageously colourful southeast side of Loaf Mountain's main summit.

At the meadow. The route goes across the meadow and then to the right.

5. This trail soon intersects a wide and obvious trail. Keep heading up the valley.

6. Things get a little confusing when you arrive in an open meadow where the trail disappears. Cross the meadow, looking for a trail to the right that goes up the headwall in front. Once you get on that trail, the remainder of the ascent to the col between Loaf and Spionkop is straightforward. Return the same way you came in, although at this point an ascent of Loaf Mountain and/ or Spionkop Ridge is almost mandatory.

Going farther to the summit of Loaf Mountain

A steep hike to the highest point in The Castle. The view from the summit is unbeatable, challenged only by that experienced from the summit of Spionkop Ridge.

DISTANCE add 4 km return	
HEIGHT GAIN add 360 m	
HIGH POINT 2640 m	
STRENUOUS steepness and length	

1. From the Loaf/Spionkop col, simply hike north and then northeast to the summit. After enjoying the outstanding view, return the same way you came in.

The ascent route up Loaf is as easy as it looks. Sandra Jacques is leaning way over to the left to balance herself against the notorious west wind. PHOTO MATTHEW CLAY.

From the summit don't forget to wander over to the northwest a short distance to get this fantastic view with Bovin Lake. PHOTO VERN DEWIT.

The intermediate high point (left) and the summit of Spionkop Ridge (right).

Closing in on the challenging summit block of Spionkop. Scrambling and route-finding required. PHOTO MATTHEW CLAY.

Going farther to the summit of Spionkop Ridge

Hike and scramble to a surreal viewpoint.

The summit view to the south features mountains in Waterton and Glacier national parks. PHOTO MATTHEW CLAY.

DISTANCE add 3.6 km return
HEIGHT GAIN add 320 m
HIGH POINT 2576 m
STRENUOUS steepness and length

1. From the Loaf/Spionkop col, hike southeast to an intermediate high point (easy hiking) and then south to the summit of Spionkop Ridge (some moderate scrambling and route-finding). This is my favourite viewpoint in all of southern Alberta. Enjoy the view and then return the same way you came in.

3 Bovin Lake

Relatively long but easy hike to a picturesque subalpine lake. Many options to extend the trip to various high points above the lake.

DISTANCE 22 km return + 1.4 km around the lake

HEIGHT GAIN 420 m

HIGH POINT 2070 m

STRENUOUS length

LATE SPRING, SUMMER, EARLY FALL

Start: About 20 km south of Pincher Creek turn right (west) onto the Waterton Shell Complex road (TWP RD 43A). Drive 9.2 km and turn left at the "Forest Reserve" sign, onto TWP RD 4-3. At 3.9 km turn left onto RGE RD 1-2A. 1.4 km turn left onto TWP RD 4-2. 5.1 km and turn right. Bovin Lake Trailhead sign is about 200 m down the road. Park on the side of the road and do not block the gate.

Difficulty: Good ATV trail all the way to the lake. Rocky in places. Bikeable, but expect to push your bike up the steeper sections and some slow going on descent.

1. Hike (or, preferably, bike) the gas road for about 4 km to its end.

2. Find the obvious trail and hike or bike about 5.7 km to a metal fence that prevents motorized vehicle access.

3. Hike a short distance to where the trail forks. Both trails lead to Bovin Lake, but the lower trail is preferred. Follow it for approximately 600 m to the lake.

4. Optional: if the water level allows it, walk around the lake in either direction to take in the different perspectives of the surrounding mountains. Return the same way you came in.

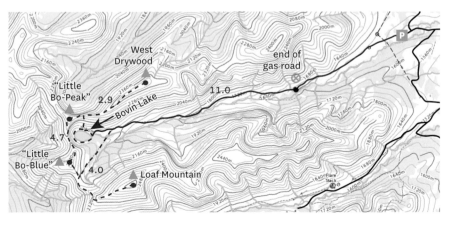

▲▲ *Loaf Mountain is the highlight on the south side of the valley.* PHOTO MATTHEW CLAY.

▲ *Bovin Lake and most of the "Bo Peak" and "Little Bo-Blue" loop route. Note the red arrow indicating the recommended ascent line.*

Going farther to "Bo Peak" and "Little Bo-Blue," above the lake (highly recommended)

An easy and fun scramble route that takes in two minor summits above the lake, humorously named by Dave McMurray. The loop is best done in a counterclockwise direction so that the more difficult sections are up-climbed, not downclimbed.

DISTANCE add 4.7 km

HEIGHT GAIN add 480 m in total

HIGH POINT 2340 m

STRENUOUS steepness and length

1. From the east end of the lake, hike around to the northwest end.

2. Turn right (north) and make your way up to the ridge via the least steep and easiest route (see photo). Persevere through this tedious section. Things improve significantly once you reach the ridge.

3. Turn left (southwest) and follow the ridge up to the red rock (argillite) summit ("Little Bo-Peak"), then down to the col and up to the second summit ("Little Bo-Blue"). Continue down the other side to the col between the second summit and Loaf Mountain. Expect some steep, loose terrain to reach the second summit and a delicate traverse across the ridge. Fun, but tread carefully!

Scott, Janina and Amber approach the scenic scramble route up "Little Bo-Blue."

4. From the col between "Little Bo-Blue" and Loaf Mountain, find the obvious trail (cutline) that goes easily back to the main trail. You will end up about 60 m from the lake. Of course, once you reach the col there is also the option to run up to the summit of Loaf Mountain (boundless energy required!).

A look at Bovin Lake and the surrounding mountains from between the two summits.

Going farther to the southwest summit of Drywood Mountain

The southwest summit of Drywood Mountain can be reached with relative ease from Bovin Lake. Expect steep terrain up to the ridge, some minor scrambling and great views.

> DISTANCE add 5.8 km return
> HEIGHT GAIN add 440 m
> HIGH POINT 2482 m
> STRENUOUS steepness and length

1. From the east end of the lake, hike around to the northwest end.

Typical easy scrambling terrain up the ridge.

2. Turn right (north) and make your way up to the ridge via the easiest and least steep route. Persevere through this tedious section. Things improve significantly once you reach the ridge.

3. Turn right (northeast) and hike/scramble to the summit, about 2 km away.

4. Return the same way you came in or, if confident in your route-finding abilities, pick a more direct line back down to the main trail. Do NOT attempt to reach the true summit of Drywood Mountain (about 4 km farther east) unless you are extremely familiar with the scramble route down the south side of that peak.

▲ *From the ridge, looking northeast along to the west summit of Drywood.*

▼ *The summit view includes a great look at multi-coloured Pincher Ridge.*

Going farther to Loaf Mountain (highly recommended)

The summit of Loaf Mountain is the highest point in the area. It sports an outstanding summit view and can be reached in about 1.5–2 hours from Bovin Lake.

DISTANCE add 8.6 km return
HEIGHT GAIN add 570 m
HIGH POINT 2640 m
STRENUOUS steepness and length

1. From Bovin Lake return along the trail about 600 m to where an obvious trail (cutline) branches off to the southwest.

2. Hike the cutline up to the col between Loaf and the unnamed summit above the lake.

3. Turn left and hike southeast, then east up to the summit of Loaf. Mostly steep hiking and no scrambling. Enjoy the view and then return the same way you came in. Alternative descent routes are possible but not recommended.

▼ *After hiking up the cutline the remainder of the route up Loaf becomes more obvious. Simply follow the ridge at the right up to the summit in the centre.* PHOTO MATTHEW CLAY.

▼▼ *Competing with Spionkop's summit view for supremacy in The Castle, Loaf's summit panorama is no slouch!* PHOTO MATTHEW CLAY.

Looking down at Bovin Lake is one of many
rewards upon reaching the summit of Loaf.
PHOTO MATTHEW CLAY.

Hiking out, surrounded by beautiful fall colours.
PHOTO VERN DEWIT.

4 North Drywood Falls

Easy gas road hike up a scenic valley to a small but interesting waterfall.

DISTANCE 8.2 km return
HEIGHT GAIN 150 m
HIGH POINT 1720 m
EASY
LATE SPRING, SUMMER, EARLY FALL, BUT ALSO A GOOD SNOWSHOE TRIP

Start: About 20 km south of Pincher Creek turn right (west) at the Butcher Lake turn-off road (TWP RD 43A). Drive 9.2 km and turn left at the "Forest Reserve" sign, onto TWP RD 4-3. Drive 2 km and turn left onto RGE RD 1-2A. Drive another 2 km and park at the locked gate (trailhead). Do not block the gate.

Difficulty: Gravel gas road approach (biking is an option), and a short section of easy trail.

1. Hike or bike about 4 km to the end of the gas road, following the trail signs at intersections.

2. A trail continues up the valley for a few hundred metres to a waterfall on your left. Again, there are trail signs to point you in the right direction. There is room to explore the falls close-up, but use extreme caution if you choose to do so.

3. The trail does go above the waterfall and is worth the minimal effort required to get there. Again, be very careful about where you choose to go when nearing the falls and the creek. Return the same way you came in.

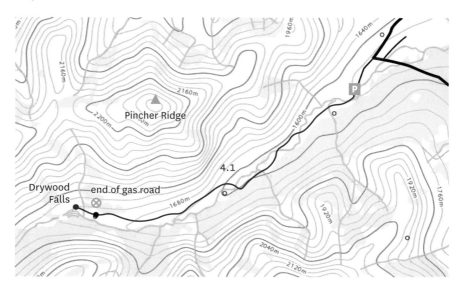

▲ Winter and spring trips can be very visually rewarding. Snowshoes or skis recommended.

◄ Maria and Brad Wolcott at the falls. PHOTO RAQUEL WOLCOTT.

*The falls. Very low water flow in early spring,
but scenic nonetheless.*

*View to the east from above the falls. Use
caution if exploring in this area.*

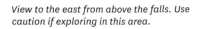

5 Victoria Ridge

One of the best trails and trips in The Castle. For scramblers, the ridge between Victoria Ridge and Victoria Peak is outstanding.

DISTANCE 25 km return
HEIGHT GAIN 1000 m
HIGH POINT 2530 m
STRENUOUS length
SUMMER, EARLY FALL

Start: About 20 km south of Pincher Creek turn right (west) at the Butcher Lake turn-off (TWP RD 43A). Drive 9.2 km and turn left at the "Forest Reserve" sign, onto TWP RD 4-3. Drive 5.5 km to the Victoria Ridge Trailhead. Park about 50 m before the locked gate.

Difficulty: 4 km along a gas road (biking recommended), followed by good trail to the summit.

1. Hike or, strongly recommended, bike the gravel road 4 km to its end. Leave your bike here.

2. Continue up the valley in a southwest direction on an obvious trail that parallels Pincher Creek below. The trail can get overgrown. As you get farther up the valley note the distinctive peak (GRO71616) that appears before you. The trail eventually traverses below that peak, high on its slopes.

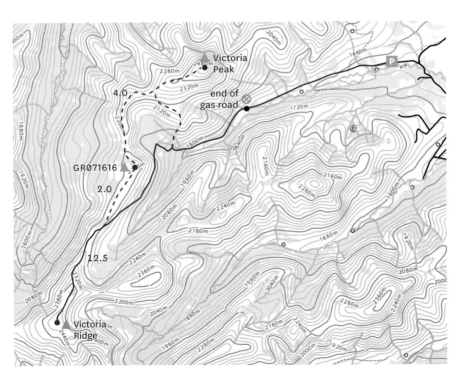

▲ Heading into the thick of things. The peak in the distance is the high point that the trail passes under. PHOTO DINAH KRUZE.

▼ Approaching the ridge, with the false summit ahead. PHOTO DINAH KRUZE.

3. A few kilometres up the valley the trail turns right, gaining elevation at a much higher rate into Thunder Basin. Watch for a point where the trail splits. Take the left fork, which turns sharply uphill. The trail then curves around the mountainside and starts traversing the distinctive peak mentioned in step 2 above. This is one of many magical moments in the hike, especially if you turn around to see the colourful form of Victoria Peak. Continue travelling south-southwest towards the ridge.

4. Already stunning views improve even more when the ridge is reached and everything to the west is revealed. Some parties may want to call this their high point, take a break, and then return the same way they came in.

5. The true summit of Victoria Ridge is about 2.7 km farther, due south. A false summit is reached first; then travel continues to the high point and a wonderful summit panorama. Return the same way you came in.

▲ *Summit view, looking down the valley you just ascended.*

Going farther to GR071616

Victoria Ridge to Victoria Peak is one of the best ridgewalk/scrambles in all of the Rockies. Halfway between the ridge and the peak sits GR071616. It is mostly a hike and a good compromise for those not ready to tackle the scrambling and route-finding challenges between GR071616 and Victoria Peak.

> **DISTANCE** add 4.4 km one way
> **HEIGHT GAIN** add approximately 200 m
> **HIGH POINT** 2296 m
> **STRENUOUS** steepness and length

1. From the summit of Victoria Ridge return the same way you came in, but when the trail descends to the right, simply stay on the ridge and follow it for several kilometres to the obvious high point (see top photo on page 34). Return the same way you came in. Don't try to take a shortcut down to the trail unless an easy route becomes visible.

▲ Hiking an alien landscape. GR071616 is the high point, just right of centre. PHOTO BOB SPIRKO.

▼ Great views of Pincher Ridge from the summit of GR071616.

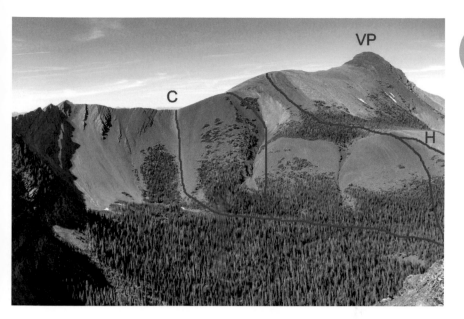

▲ *Some potential routes back down to the trail after descending some of Victoria Peak. VP Victoria Peak. H high route from the shoulder. C col. V valley.*

▼ *The exciting ridge between the GR and the summit of Victoria Peak at the right. We did the traverse in the opposite direction. PHOTO MARK NUGARA.*

Going farther to Victoria Peak

A spectacular ridge to a spectacular summit, requiring good route-finding and some moderate scrambling. Recommended only for scramblers.

> **DISTANCE** add 4 km to the summit from GRO71616
>
> **HEIGHT GAIN** add approximately 520 m
>
> **HIGH POINT** 2587 m
>
> **STRENUOUS** steepness and length

1. From GRO71616 simply follow the ridge generally northward. Staying directly on the ridge is not always an option. A few detours over to the left will be necessary. Try to return to the ridge as much as possible. If you encounter anything more than moderate scrambling, back up and find an easier route.

2. As you traverse the ridge be sure to check out the possible descent routes emanating from the shoulder of Victoria Peak (see top photo on page 35).

3. From the low col southwest of the summit it's a slightly more tedious grind to the summit, but very straightforward. Again, try to note a good spot on the southwest shoulder of the peak to use as a descent route that goes more directly down to the trail.

4. After taking in an awesome summit view descend the way you came, back down to the shoulder and then turn left (southeast) and route-find your way down to the trail and out. It is also possible to descend to the col and then down, but that route is steeper.

Late September trips can yield some of the most extraordinary colours you may ever see. PHOTO VERN DEWIT.

6 Prairie Bluff

A very enjoyable route that takes in one of the smallest but most interesting mountains of The Castle East.

DISTANCE 16.6 km

HEIGHT GAIN 715 m

HIGH POINT 2255 m

STRENUOUS steepness and length

SUMMER, EARLY FALL

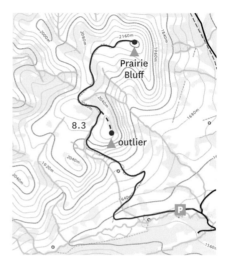

Start: About 20 km south of Pincher Creek turn right (west) at the Butcher Lake turn-off (TWP RD 43A). Drive 9.2 km and turn left at the "Forest Reserve" sign, onto TWP RD 4-3. Drive 5.5 km to the Victoria Ridge Trailhead. Park about 50 m before the locked gate.

Difficulty: Gravel roads, faint trails and steep scree. Some route-finding necessary. Biking the 3 km approach will save time.

1. Hike or bike the main gas road for 1.6 km and turn right, onto a subsidiary gas road.

2. Hike this road for about 1.4 km, going straight and up at the first intersection, until the road curves sharply to the west.

3. Leave the road here and follow a trail (made by cattle) going in a northeast direction. The goal is to ascend the outlier in front and find the trail that runs right to left up the side of the outlier (see top photo on page 38).

4. Find the trail and follow it up and around the left side of the outlier. The trail eventually swings around to the right. Do not descend into the drainage on the left. Instead, stay on the side of the hill above the drainage and follow it up until you intersect one of the main gas roads.

5. For an optional visit to the summit of the outlier you have just ascended, turn right onto the gas road and follow it past a gas well and up to the high point.

6. Otherwise, turn left onto the grey gas road that abruptly turns into a red, argillite road. Follow this winding road, passing another gas well on the left side and then up the wide ridge to the summit. Return the same way you came in. For some variety you can follow the main gas road all the way back down to the valley and out. This is a slightly longer route, but straightforward and very easy.

▲ This is the outlier of Prairie Bluff that provides the ascent route. Note the faint trail on the side of the outlier near the left. That's the route up.

▼ On the red argillite gas road, looking to the summit. The road goes around to the left and then up to the summit.

▲ *The final slog to the summit features a terrific view of Victoria Peak.*

▼ *The road gets plowed throughout the winter, creating huge snowbanks, even in mid-April.*

THE CASTLE WEST

The photo at the western plateau of Table Mountain that everyone stops to take. A few steps in the wrong direction and you get to experience first-hand what acceleration of 9.81 m/s² feels like!
PHOTO MATTHEW CLAY.

7 Mount Albert Loop

A very pleasant hike through forest to several fine viewpoints over The Castle area.

DISTANCE 3.8 km one way

HEIGHT GAIN 300 m

HIGH POINT 1620 m

MODERATE

LATE SPRING, SUMMER, FALL

Start: From the Pincher Creek roundabout turn west onto Highway 507. Drive 10 km and turn left (south) onto Highway 775. Follow this road for 8 km to Beauvais Lake Park. Once in the park, turn right ("Homestead Group Use") and follow the road to its end, at the Beaver Creek Day Use Area.

Difficulty: Good trails most of the way, with several steep sections.

1. The Mount Albert trail starts at the end of the parking lot to the right. Given the proliferation of trails and trail signs, a detailed description is unnecessary. Follow the trail for a short distance, over a bridge and to the first intersection. Turn right and then left onto the Homestead Group User road.

2. At the next intersection turn left onto the main trail. Follow the trail, using the signs to "Upper Smith Homestead." Take a brief detour to check out the remains of the homestead.

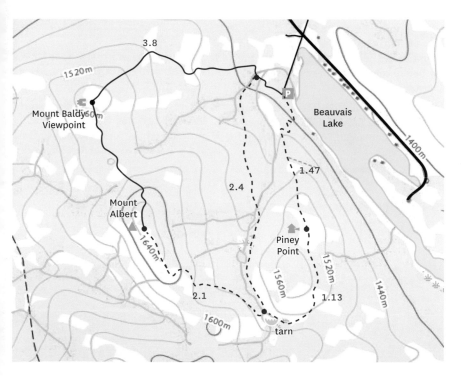

The Dewit kids hike through the meadows at Upper Smith Homestead. The homestead is in the centre. PHOTO VERN DEWIT.

3. From the Upper Smith Homestead continue on the trail and then on to "Viewpoint Mount Baldy." Enjoy the first summit of the day before continuing on towards Mount Albert.

4. Although a trail from Mount Baldy to Mount Albert is not depicted on the map, a good trail does exist. Follow it down and

towards Mount Albert. Once you are on the slopes of Albert, the terrain does get steeper and the trail becomes faint for a few short sections. There are orange-diamond markers to guide you.

5. Eventually you will intersect the Mount Albert trail. Turn right and follow it steeply to the summit.

6. There are three options for return. 1. The same way you came in. 2. Via the Mount Albert trail — easy to follow and well signed. 3. The Loop route as described next.

The Dewits at the Mount Baldy viewpoint. PHOTO VERN DEWIT.

▲ Niko and Kaycie Dewit check out Mount Albert. PHOTO VERN DEWIT.

▼ Brad Wolcott and daughter Maria enjoying their day on the mountain. PHOTO RAQUEL WOLCOTT.

Making a loop of it

A steep descent off Mount Albert and then more pleasant forest walking with two options for finishing the loop.

DISTANCE 4.5–4.7 km one way
HEIGHT GAIN add 80 m

1. From the summit of Mount Albert, continue hiking southeastward, watching for a point where the trail turns sharply left. The steepest section on the descent comes soon after. Stay on the trail, crossing a creek just before reaching a major intersection. It's 2.1 km from the summit to this point.

2. Decision time. The left fork stays in the valley and offers interesting marsh scenery. The right fork skirts a shallow tarn and eventually goes to the high point, Piney Point. That fork offers decent views of the area, though inferior to those from Albert. Both routes end back at the Beaver Creek Day Use parking lot. Finish the trip with an optional short walk along the south shore of Beauvais Lake.

▼ *The marsh section if you took the left fork.* PHOTO VERN DEWIT.

▶ *Niko and Kaycie descend one of the steeper sections on along the loop route. It's steeper than it looks.* PHOTO VERN DEWIT.

▼ *The shallow tarn if you took the right fork.*

TABLE MOUNTAIN AND WHISTLER MOUNTAIN

Table and Whistler almost deserve a section of their own. They are part of the same massif and it is therefore possible to go up one mountain and down the other, taking in numerous high points along the way. If you intend to complete this awesome but very strenuous traverse, it is a good idea to leave a second vehicle or bike at the other trailhead. The recommended direction is to start at Table and finish at Whistler. A detailed description is provided for that route. Read the Whistler Mountain description to find out where to leave the other vehicle or bike. Of course, most will simply choose to ascend each mountain individually — this area is worth multiple visits!

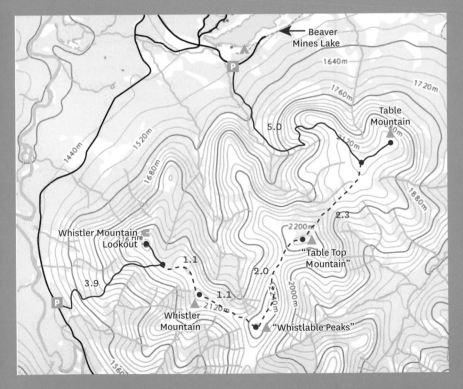

◄ *The snowy Flathead Range provides a stunning backdrop on Table Mountain.*

8 Table Mountain

One of the more challenging trips in the book, but incredibly scenic and extremely enjoyable.

DISTANCE 10 km return
HEIGHT GAIN 740 m
HIGH POINT 2225 m
STRENUOUS steepness
LATE SPRING, SUMMER, FALL

Start: From Pincher Creek, drive west on Highway 507. Turn left onto Highway 774 and drive 15 km. Turn left onto Beaver Mines Lake road. Drive 5.5 km to the signed Table Mountain parking lot on the right side of the road. There is additional parking if you turn left before the normal parking.

Difficulty: Good trail all the way, but long sections of steep, rocky, loose terrain and scree. Some minor scrambling required. Wear good hiking boots. Hiking poles are useful.

1. As the trail basically goes from trailhead to summit, a detailed description is not necessary, but studying the trailhead map carefully may help. Follow the trail through forest, up to near treeline, across the mountainside, then up the major ascent drainage to the western summit (plateau). For the second half of this part, **always** follow the dark orange trail markers and the dark orange painted circles on rocks for the easiest line. Other routes are possible but steeper and more difficult.

2. Up high, note the striking multi-layered (coloured) rock band that seems to guard the western summit. This band is one of the scenic highlights of the day and worthy of exploration. In fact, you can traverse left (northeast) along the base of it and then scramble up through a weakness near the end.

Aurore Kurc stops by a dead tree to enjoy the surroundings. PHOTO MATTHEW HOBBS.

Enjoying the impressive red argillite rock band below the western plateau. The weakness up the rock band lies to the left. PHOTO MARK NUGARA.

3. Exploring the western summit is optional but highly recommended. There are great views of Beaver Mines Lake, and the vertiginous drop down the north face is breathtaking — don't get too close to the edge on windy days!

4. Continue following the trail east, then southeast to an intermediate high point, then northeast through a large stand of larches to the summit. Enjoy the terrific view, especially looking back to the western plateau. You will need to wander down the ridge, heading west, for a short distance to get a good view of Beaver Mines Lake. Return the same way you came in.

From the western plateau the route to the summit unfolds with ease. PHOTO MATTHEW HOBBS.

► *The most popular photo op in The Castle. Matt Hobbs sensibly stands a good distance away from the edge.* PHOTO AURORE KURC.

▼ *Part of the summit view to the north.* PHOTO MATTHEW HOBBS.

Table Top Mountain (right), as seen from the ascent slopes of Table. The easiest route starts from the high point to the left (not seen in the photo). **PHOTO MATTHEW CLAY.**

Going farther to "Table Top Mountain"

If the summit of Table Mountain wasn't enough, this extension to a slightly higher summit (unofficially named "Table Top Mountain") to the south is great for some extra exercise and continued awesome views.

DISTANCE 4.6 km return

HEIGHT GAIN add 320 m in total

HIGH POINT 2270 m

STRENUOUS length

1. From the summit of Table, return to the intermediate high point. Then, instead of turning west, veer south, then south-southwest to the summit of Table Top, about 2.3 km away. You will lose about 120 m and gain 200 m en route. The forest between the peaks is light and easy to get through. Return the same way you came in, or for those with boundless energy and daylight to spare, continue on to Whistable Peaks to the south and possibly all the way to Whistler Mountain.

Summit view from Table Top. Don't forget to wear your brightly coloured clothing! **PHOTO MARK NUGARA.**

The scenic ridge from Table Top to Whistable Peaks at the left. PHOTO MATTHEW CLAY.

Going farther to "Whistable Peaks"

This extension makes for a long day, but once again the ridgewalking is superb.

DISTANCE add 4 km return from Table Top
HEIGHT GAIN add 280 m in total
HIGH POINT 2280 m
STRENUOUS steepness and length

1. From Table Top Mountain, follow the ridge south-southwest and south for approximately 2 km to the high point that is the farthest south. There are three closely spaced high points here. The entire ridge is generally off-trail hiking, with a couple of easy scrambling moves. Return the same way you came in or continue the trip over to Whistler Mountain.

At the first of the three high points with the objective just right of centre. PHOTO MATTHEW CLAY.

Going farther to Whistler Mountain

The ultimate extension. Guaranteed to leave you fully satiated, dead-on-your feet or both!

DISTANCE add 6 km to the Whistler Mountain trailhead

HEIGHT GAIN add 200 m in total

HIGH POINT 2214 m

STRENUOUS steepness and length

1. From Whistable Peak, hike about 1.1 km west to the next high point. It is treed, lower than Whistable, and yet is the official summit of Whistler Mountain.

2. Hike 600 m northwest to the next high point. The red argillite scenery along this stretch is fantastic. Many consider this point to be the summit of Whistler Mountain.

3. The next destination is the former Whistler Lookout. Hike 500 m downhill in a southwest direction to a low point. Note that the descent trail off the mountain is found here. Hike another 550 m uphill in a northwest direction to the former lookout, now just the remnants of its base. Enjoy the view and take a break to recuperate for the remainder of the trip.

4. Return to the low point and find the trail on the south side of the ridge.

5. Follow this trail all the way to the valley bottom and the Castle River gravel road. Turn right and hike 440 m to the parking area, where hopefully a second vehicle or a bicycle awaits. If not, it's about an 8 km hike on the Castle River road and then on the Beaver Mines Lake road back to the Table Mountain parking lot.

Looking west to treed Whistler Mountain.
PHOTO MATTHEW CLAY.

The main descent trail off Whistler Mountain.
PHOTO MATTHEW CLAY.

9 Whistler Mountain Fire Lookout

Pleasant hike to a great viewpoint, with many options to reach other high points.

DISTANCE 7.8 km return

HEIGHT GAIN 750 m

HIGH POINT 2160 m

MODERATE

LATE SPRING, SUMMER, FALL

Start: From Pincher Creek, drive west on Highway 507 and then turn left onto Highway 774. Drive for approximately 15 km and turn left on Beaver Mines Road. In 3.7 km, turn right and drive a rough, potholed road for 5.7 km to where the road is blocked. A potential creek crossing is encountered 600 m along the road and may stop progress in times of high water. Walking to the trailhead from this point adds 10.2 km to the trip and you will have to ford the creek.

Difficulty: Good trail all the way to the former fire lookout. Rough trails and sometimes no trail to other high points. Some minor scrambling may be required.

1. Hike 440 m farther down the road and find the signed trailhead on the left side. From this point on, the clearly defined trail takes you all the way up the mountain. There are some sections that are relentlessly steep. The trail eventually becomes a very picturesque red argillite path, lined with dead trees.

2. Upon reaching the ridge (col), turn left and hike about 550 m up to the high point of the ridge. The only remnant of the old

Bob Spirko hikes the superb red argillite trail on the upper section of the trail. PHOTO DINAH KRUZE.

fire lookout is its concrete foundation. Return the same way you came in or better yet continue the trip to the summit of Whistler Mountain — highly recommended, at least to the first high point.

See page 47 for map.

Going farther to Whistler Mountain

For a better view and some very cool red argillite rock formations, the summit of Whistler Mountain is close by and doesn't require a great deal of time and effort.

▼ *The view from the lookout includes Beaver Mines Lake and Table Mountain.*

▼▼ *Excellent red argillite perch for Sandra Jacques at the first high point.* PHOTO MATTHEW CLAY.

DISTANCE add 2–3.2 km return from the fire lookout

HEIGHT GAIN add 120 m

HIGH POINT 2190 m

STRENUOUS

1. Return to the col and then hike east, up to the next high point. This is not the official summit of Whistler Mountain but provides an amazing view.

2. If desired, continue following the ridge southeastward to the mostly treed true summit. The motivation here may be to continue the trip to "Whistable Peak," "Table Top Mountain" and/or Table Mountain. A detailed description, in reverse, is given in the Table Mountain write-up. Return the same way you came in or continue the trek.

▼▼ Looking east along the ridge. Whistler Mountain is the treed point at the right. "Whistable Peak" is the rounded bump at the left. PHOTO MATTHEW CLAY.

▼ Some of the terrific scenery between the first high point and Whistler Mountain.

10 Carbondale Hill

An easy road hike to a fine viewpoint. Biking all or part of the trail is possible.

DISTANCE 8 km return

HEIGHT GAIN 450 m

HIGH POINT 1798 m

MODERATE

LATE SPRING, SUMMER, FALL

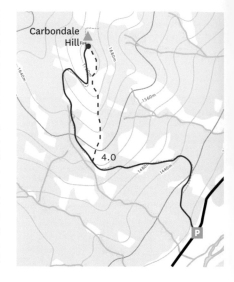

Start: From Pincher Creek, drive west on Highway 507 and then turn left onto Highway 774. Drive approximately 15.3 km and turn right onto RGE RD 3-0 (Lynx Creek). Follow the road for approximately 3 km to an unsigned, gated trailhead on the west side of the road. Park on the side of the road, without blocking the gate. Note that the access road is closed from from Dec. 1 to May 15, necessitating an extra 1.2 km of walking (one way) to get to the trailhead.

Difficulty: Wide fire lookout road all the way, with the option for off-trail travel. Note there is an active fire lookout at the top. Be respectful, considerate and polite to the residents.

1. Hike past the gate and up you go. The fire road is easy to follow all the way to the summit. About 30 minutes up (2 km), look for a minor trail veering off to the left that goes to a terrific viewpoint. Great place for a quick break.

2. Either continue along the road to the summit, or, a short distance farther up the road from the viewpoint, leave the trail and veer right and up, onto the south slopes. Gain the south ridge and follow it north. This route offers some variety and almost immediate views. The ridge does intersect the road a couple of times en route.

3. Regardless of the route you took to the summit, enjoy the panoramic view. Do not go onto the lookout unless invited by the lookout person. Return via the road or the south ridge. If you took the south ridge up, the road is an easy and pleasant alternative going down.

▲ Near the start of the south face/ridge route.

▼ The south ridge offers terrific views of the east side of Carbondale that are not seen from the road route.

11 North Kootenay Pass

A long bike/hike to a remote and breathtaking pass near the Alberta/ BC boundary.

DISTANCE 22–29 km return

HEIGHT GAIN 650 m

HIGH POINT 2075 m

STRENUOUS length

SUMMER, EARLY FALL

Start: From Pincher Creek, drive west on Highway 507 and then turn left onto Highway 774. Drive approximately 15.3 km and turn right onto RGE RD 3-0 (Lynx Creek). Follow the road for 1.8 km and turn left. In 7.8 km turn left onto TWP RD 6-0 and drive 2.5 km to an open area with a kiosk. Without a 4×4 and high-clearance vehicle the trip starts here. With a 4×4 it is possible to drive about 4 km farther up the road, to the trailhead, but it's a slow, rough drive. Some will drive 3.3 km, park in an open area and then hike about 700 m to the trailhead.

Difficulty: Good ATV trail all the way to the pass. Two unbridged creek crossings required (bring your runners). If you are parking at the kiosk, biking to the trailhead and beyond is strongly recommended. Strong bikers could pedal almost to the pass.

1. From the kiosk, hike the road about 4 km to the signed trailhead. The trail from here is very easy to follow. The first few stream crossings are bridged.

2. Go past the turnoff to MacDonald Pass, about 3.8 km from the trailhead. Continue on the North Kootenay Pass trail, soon reaching an unbridged stream crossing. By early summer, the crossing will probably be less than knee-deep.

3. Continue to the next crossing of the Carbondale River. If you are cycling, this is one place you could leave your bike. Cross the river and continue all the way to North Kootenay Pass, ignoring a prominent trail that veers off to the right and up at one point and other minor trails along the way. The high point of the pass is about 300 m past a plaque on a huge boulder in honour of explorer Thomas Blakiston. Return the same way you came in (after completing the highly recommended run up "North Kootenay Point").

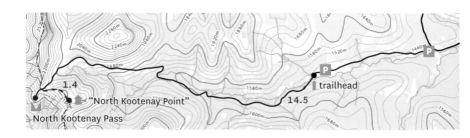

1.4
"North Kootenay Point"
North Kootenay Pass
trailhead
14.5

▲ The official trailhead. Note that this is about 4 km from the kiosk.

▼ Dave McMurray and Brad Wolcott are getting close to the pass.

Going farther to "North Kootenay Point"

You've made it this far — why not go for a sweet summit that's easier to reach than appearances dictate. Great viewpoint!

DISTANCE add 1.6–2.4 km return
HEIGHT GAIN add 175 m
HIGH POINT 2240 m
STRENUOUS steepness

1. Return the way you came in for a short distance until a good place to the right appears where you can make your way onto the ridge.

Brad and Dave at North Kootenay Pass.

2. Once on the ridge of the objective, simply follow it to the summit, where in addition to a magnificent view, you will also find an Alberta/BC boundary marker. Return the same way you came in.

3. Optional and highly recommended: a slightly lower high point sits about 400 m to the southeast and provides a view that is superior in some ways to that of the Point. Go there and then return the same way you came in.

FACING PAGE FROM TOP *"North Kootenay Point" (just right of centre), as seen from North Kootenay Pass. The route follows the obvious ridgeline from left to right; Dave hikes the splendid open terrain of the ridge between North Kootenay Point and the lower high point; Brad surveys the area before finishing the ascent to the lower high point. The peak to the right is Hollebeke Mountain and can be reached from here but is considerably more challenging than North Kootenay Point.*

12 Southfork Lakes

A relentlessly steep hike to three beautiful alpine lakes. Excellent during larch season.

DISTANCE 10 km return

HEIGHT GAIN 625 m

HIGH POINT 2025 m

STRENUOUS steepness

SUMMER, EARLY FALL

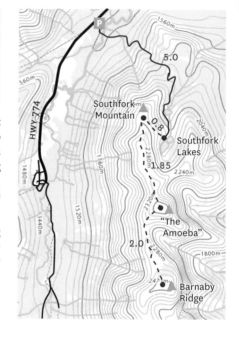

Start: From Pincher Creek, drive west on Highway 507 and then turn left onto Highway 774. Drive approximately 23 km (5.5 km past the South Syncline Staging Area) and turn left on a signed road, 5003. The small parking area is a short distance down the road.

Difficulty: Good trail all the way, but long sections of very steep terrain. Fording the West Castle River may not be possible for early season attempts.

The first lake. The trail goes around the right side. PHOTO MATTHEW CLAY.

1. Hip-waders are a good idea for the river crossing and can be put on at the car. Hike down the ATV trail, ignoring the first right-hand turn and then taking the second right, where the hiking sign is. Follow the trail down to the banks of the West Castle River. Note the location of the trail sign on the other side of the river.

2. Ford the river. This is usually easier about 50 m downstream.

3. Resume travel on the other side, taking a left turn at a trail sign in short order.

4. There are no intersections from here on in — just a very steep hike (with over 600 m of elevation gain total) up the west face and then easier travel along the north ridge to the first of the three Southfork Lakes.

5. From the head of the first lake, follow the trail around the lake's right shore and then up to the second and third lakes.

6. Perhaps the most interesting feature of the upper lakes is the rock wall between them. It is possible to walk the wall and cross the stream that drains the third lake into the second. Going around the third lake in a clockwise direction will require a little bushwhacking but has terrific views at the end. Getting to the far end of the lake is much easier travelling counterclockwise.

7. After exploring the lakes, return the same way you came in or head up to the summit of Southfork Mountain.

Going farther to the summit of Southfork Mountain

A steep and trail-less slog up to an official summit with a great view. Highly recommended for those comfortable on this type of terrain, and also recommended during larch season.

DISTANCE add 1.6 km return

HEIGHT GAIN add 300 m

HIGH POINT 2350 m

STRENUOUS steepness

1. The best place to start the ascent is the open rocky area above and between the second and third lakes. Follow the line of least resistance up the increasingly steep and larch-filled slopes. Follow your nose to the cairned summit. Return the same way you came in or continue on.

The second lake. The third is just beyond.
PHOTO MATTHEW CLAY.

► *Looking up the ascent slopes to Southfork Mountain. Pick the easiest line up.* PHOTO MATTHEW CLAY.

▼ *Looking back at the upper lakes. Note the rock bridge between the lakes.* PHOTO MATTHEW CLAY.

▼▼ *The summit view includes Mount Haig and Gravenstafel Peak.* PHOTO MATTHEW CLAY.

Going farther to the summit of "The Amoeba"

An awesome extension of Southfork Mountain. Fantastic ridgewalking, with some minor scrambling, and terrific views throughout.

DISTANCE	add 3.7 km return
HEIGHT GAIN	add 150 m
HIGH POINT	2465 m
STRENUOUS	steepness and length

The only challenging terrain between Southfork and "The Amoeba." It's easier than it looks, but still a scramble. PHOTO MATTHEW CLAY.

From near the summit of Southfork, the route to "The Amoeba" (centre) and Barnaby Ridge (distant right of centre) is obvious and straightforward. PHOTO MATTHEW CLAY.

1. Simply follow the ridge southeastward, picking the line of least resistance throughout. Some minor scrambling is required.

2. "The Amoeba" is the first significant summit reached, composed almost entirely of bright red argillite. It is over 100 vertical metres higher than Southfork Mountain, and thus its summit views are far more comprehensive. Many will call it a day here and return the same way they came in.

Going farther to the summit of Barnaby Ridge

More of the same awesome ridgewalking, with wonderful views of "The Amoeba." Note this makes for a very long (and rewarding) day with a significant amount of elevation gain.

DISTANCE add 4 km return from "The Amoeba" (19.3 km in total for the day)

HEIGHT GAIN add 460 m from "The Amoeba" (1850 m in total for the day)

HIGH POINT 2475 m

STRENUOUS steepness and length

Looking down the precipitous east side of Barnaby Ridge after passing "The Amoeba." PHOTO MARK NUGARA.

Chillin' near the summit of "The Amoeba." PHOTO MARK NUGARA.

1. If you are up for the challenge, continue following the ups and downs of the ridge in a general southeast direction to the highest point of Barnaby Ridge. Going to the lower high point southwest of the summit offers great views to the ridge you just traversed. Return the same way you came in. There is a more direct route down to the gravel road that parallels the West Castle River, but it may be difficult to find if you haven't come up that way. On return it is possible to bypass "The Amoeba."

▲ From the summit of "The Amoeba" the route to Barnaby Ridge is obvious and straightforward. PHOTO MATTHEW CLAY.

◄ Interesting and varied scenery throughout the traverse.

▼ From the lower summit of Barnaby Ridge it's a long but super scenic traverse back to Southfork and the lakes. PHOTO MARK NUGARA.

CASTLE MOUNTAIN RESORT

Primarily a winter destination for downhill skiers, the Castle Mountain Resort area has also become a gold mine of terrific summer hikes, all starting from the resort parking lot. The described four trails can be completed individually or in combination. For example, Paradise Lake followed by Haig Ridge, or Haig Lake followed by Gravenstafel Peak. Reaching the summit of statuesque Mount Haig via the Haig/Gravenstafel col will undoubtedly be a real "feather in the cap" for strong hikers and scramblers.

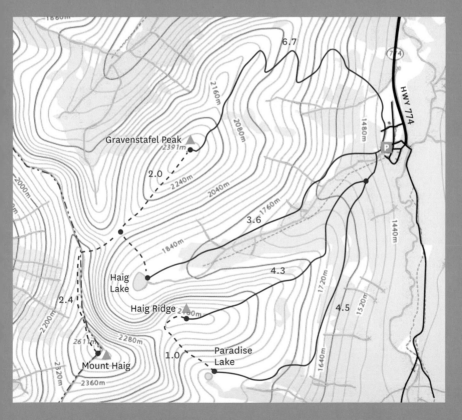

◄ *Dave McMurray on one of the numerous high points on Haig Ridge. An unusual amount of snow for early October.*

13 Gravenstafel Peak

A lengthy hike up ski runs and access roads to an outstanding viewpoint.

DISTANCE 13.4 km return

HEIGHT GAIN 940 m

HIGH POINT 2389 m

STRENUOUS length

SUMMER, EARLY FALL

Start: From Pincher Creek, drive west on Highway 507. Turn left onto Highway 774. Drive 27 km and turn right, into the Castle Mountain ski resort. Park near the main building.

Difficulty: Wide, gently graded gravel roads most of the way. Steeper near the summit.

1. From the parking lot, hike west past the main building and turn right, passing the ski lifts.

2. Turn left at the first intersection and start the long trek up access roads and ski runs towards the top. The summit is visible right away and you should note its general location. A detailed description is unnecessary. Follow your nose, always staying on the widest and most obvious roads. Access roads are preferable to ski runs. Shortcutting up step ski runs can be self-defeating and sometimes slick on the grassy slopes.

The route stays on the north side of the mountain.

3. Nearing the summit there are two routes to the top. The easiest one continues on a trail behind a service shed, going almost all the way to the top. A more challenging route gains the ridge on the right immediately and follows it to the top. Some route-finding on steep terrain will be necessary. Return the same way you came in. Completing a loop route via the Gravenstafel/Haig col and then Haig Lake is certainly a possibility for those who are comfortable with route-finding their way down steep slopes to the lake, but this route is not recommended. Refer to the Haig Lake North trip for the recommended route.

See page 71 for map.

FACING PAGE FROM TOP Nothing better than a road of red argillite to ascend! Approaching the upper section of the ascent. The service shed is the small dot near the left. The ridge can also be ascended head-on. PHOTO MATTHEW CLAY.; *Mount Haig and Haig Lake, as seen from the near the summit.* PHOTO MATTHEW CLAY; *Excellent view to the northwest.* PHOTO MATTHEW CLAY.

▼ *Behind the main building. The obvious road to the right is the way up. The summit can be seen near the left.*

14 Haig Lake North

Easy hike to a small, secluded lake under the awesome north face of Mount Haig.

DISTANCE 7.2 km return
HEIGHT GAIN 420 m
HIGH POINT 1790 m
MODERATE
SUMMER, EARLY FALL

Start: From Pincher Creek, drive west on Highway 507. Turn left onto Highway 774. Drive 27 km and turn right, into the Castle Mountain ski resort. Park near the main building.

Difficulty: Good trail all the way.

1. From the parking lot, hike west past the main building and turn left, passing the ski lifts, as you hike up the gravel road (Haig Way).

2. Approaching a bridge over Haig Creek, look for a sign for Haig Lake North. If you cross the creek, you have gone too far.

3. The trail gains elevation right away, switchbacking across a ski run.

4. After a big chunk of elevation is gained, the trail then merges with a very gently graded ski run, heading northwest. Follow this trail (eventually becoming a single track), to Haig Lake. There is a little bit of elevation loss as the trail veers left and down to the lake.

5. Perhaps the most interesting feature of the lake is the small glacier melting out its remaining years at the south end of the lake. Go check it out, but do not go under it, because of rockfall.

6. Return the same way you came in or for some variety follow the signed Haig Lake South route back. Going up to Gravenstafel Peak is also an option.

See page 71 for map.

The imposing form of Mount Haig is one of the highlights of the trip.

▲ *View towards Gravenstafel Peak from the south side of the lake. Note the glacier at the left.*

▲ *Looking up to the Haig/Gravenstafel col. The least steep route goes directly to the second lowest point, right of centre.*

Going farther to Gravenstafel Peak

For scramblers and able hikers comfortable on very steep, loose terrain without a trail. Views and scenery are outstanding.

DISTANCE add 4 km return to Haig Lake; add 6.8 km for descent via Gravenstafel Peak

HEIGHT GAIN add 600 m

HIGH POINT 2389 m

STRENUOUS steepness and length

75

▲ The terrain around the col is littered with amazing lichen-covered rock.

▼ Looking down the north ridge descent route. Note the service shed and the roads that switchback down the mountain.

1. From the lake, work your way up steep, loose slopes to the Haig/Gravenstafel col (ridge). A direct route to the low point or a scree gully to the right is your best bet.

2. From the col follow the ridge north to the summit. There are several false summits along the way and over 300 m of elevation gain, so expect to take some time.

3. Either return the same the way you came in or take the recommended alternative descent route as follows.

4. Descend the north ridge, looking for a trail that goes down to a service shed and then onto the ski access roads. If you stay on the ridge, a few moves of scrambling on steep terrain will be required.

5. Once on the road, follow it all the way down the mountain to the parking lot.

Going farther to Mount Haig

Summit the highest official mountain in The Castle West. For scramblers and strong hikers comfortable on steep, loose terrain with some minor exposure.

DISTANCE add 4.8 km return

HEIGHT GAIN add 820 m

HIGH POINT 2618 m

STRENUOUS steepness and length

1. From the lake, work your way up steep, loose slopes to the Haig/Gravenstafel col (ridge). A direct route to the low point is your best bet.

2. Follow the steep ridge southwest to a minor high point (scrambling and minor exposure) and then south and east to the summit. Take in one of the best summit views in the area and then return the same way you came in. Alternative descent routes are possible but not recommended.

From near the Haig/Gravenstafel col, the route to the minor high point is obvious.

Matt Hobbs starts up the long but scenic ridge to the summit. PHOTO MATTHEW CLAY.

Matt Hobbs near the summit of Mount Haig. Note colourful Haig Lake far below. PHOTO MATTHEW CLAY.

15 Haig Ridge

A terrific larch-season trip with fantastic views of Mount Haig and others.

DISTANCE 8.6 km return

HEIGHT GAIN 770 m

HIGH POINT 2186 m

STRENUOUS steepness

SUMMER, EARLY FALL

Start: From Pincher Creek, drive west on Highway 507. Turn left onto Highway 774. Drive 27 km and turn right, into the Castle Mountain ski resort. Park near the main building.

Difficulty: Good trail most of the way, but there are steep, rocky sections higher up which lack a trail and require route-finding to the summit.

1. From the parking lot, hike west past the main building and turn left, passing the ski lifts, as you hike up the gravel road (Haig Way) to trail signs before a bridge.

2. Follow the Haig Ride signs and trail markers up access roads and ski runs.

3. At the top the ski lift, look for a Haig Ridge trail sign and continue up steeper and rocky terrain.

4. Eventually the trail/road ends. Continue going up the ridge in a southwest direction, through stands of larches and then onto the high point. Enjoy the view and then return the same way you came in or make it a loop route via Paradise Lake.

See page 71 for map.

Haig Ridge and Mount Haig, as seen from the parking lot.

79

Loop route via Paradise Lake

Why not add to an already terrific trip by visiting a small but beautiful lake below Mount Haig?

> DISTANCE 5.5 km from summit to parking lot
>
> Off-trail travel with route-finding and steep slopes to descend. Note that if your intention is to visit both Haig Ridge and Paradise Lake, the recommended route is to go to Paradise Lake first, as described for that trip.
>
> STRENUOUS steepness and length

1. From the summit descend southwest to the low col between Haig Ridge and the northeast ridge of Mount Haig.

2. Turn left (southeast) and descend very steep slopes down to the lake. There is a gully of colourful, step-like rock that is enjoyable to look at and descend if it is dry.

Don't expect yellow larches and snow at the same time. A freak early October snowstorm rendered this one of the most scenic trips I've ever done.

3. After checking out the lake, hike east, down the valley, staying more to the left side than the right. You will always want to be on the north side of the drainage emanating from Paradise Lake.

4. Find the trail and follow it alongside the drainage for a short distance. This trail then veers left and winds through the forest, eventually intersecting a wide ski trail / gravel road. Turn right, onto this gravel road, and follow it easily back to the parking area.

▲ *Looking down to Paradise Lake.*

▼ *This very random white rock on the hill at the east end of the lake makes for a good viewpoint.*

81

16 Paradise Lake

Similar to Haig Lake, with the option to complete a loop route via Haig Ridge. Awesome colours around larch season.

DISTANCE 9 km return

HEIGHT GAIN 435 m

HIGH POINT 1838 m

MODERATE

SUMMER, EARLY FALL

Start: From Pincher Creek, drive west on Highway 507. Turn left onto Highway 774. Drive 27 km and turn right, into the Castle Mountain ski resort. Park near the main building.

Difficulty: Good trail most of the way, with some route-finding and trail-less travel near the lake. Note that early in the season the lake can be little more than a big puddle or completely snow-covered.

1. From the parking lot, hike west past the main building and turn left, passing the ski lifts as you hike up the gravel road (Haig Way) to trail signs before a bridge.

2. Hike the wide ski/access road, following the signs for Paradise Lake. Stay left when you reach the Haig Ridge sign, continuing the long traverse across the east side of Mount Haig.

3. Eventually the road turns more to the right and gains a large amount of elevation up steep terrain.

4. When the road levels out a little and starts to straighten, look to the left for a marked trail heading into the forest. This may or may not be signed and is easy to miss when the sign isn't there.

FACING PAGE FROM TOP Waterfall scenery abounds on late spring trips. Natasha Rajcevic stays very still while I take a long-exposure photo! The milky turquoise waters of Paradise Lake, from its south side.

▼ *Pat and Gord Hobbs ("Grandma" and "Grandpa"), with their eldest "grandchild" (Crux the dog), enjoy a terrific rest spot along the way.* PHOTO MATTHEW HOBBS.

5. This new trail winds through the forest, eventually reaching the drainage that empties Paradise Lake. Do not cross the drainage. Instead, stay on a trail on the north side of the drainage, heading west.

6. This trail eventually disappears, but the route to the lake is obvious and easy.

7. At the lake, a hill on the east side makes for a fine viewpoint. Return the same way you came in.

See page 71 for map.

Going farther to Haig Ridge

A fantastic loop route via Haig Ridge, but very steep going up.

> DISTANCE add 5.3 km
> HEIGHT GAIN add 350 m
> STRENUOUS steepness and length

1. Hike around the west side of the lake and ascend increasingly steep scree slopes in a west-northwest direction towards the col between Mount Haig and Haig Ridge.

2. A water-worn drainage about halfway up to the left provides beautiful rock scenery and staircase-like footing — excellent!

Hiking around the west side of the lake to the ascent slopes and the ascent gully to the Mount Haig/Haig Ridge col. The staircase rock trends to the left, but eventually you will want to turn right, towards the summit of Haig Ridge.

Continue up the staircase for a surprisingly long stretch and then traverse right, towards the col.

3. Regardless of the route you take to the col, once there turn northeast and hike up to the high point of Haig Ridge and a wonderful view.

4. Returning the same way you came is certainly a possibility, but descending the Haig Ridge route is the preferred option.

5. Follow the ridge down in a northeast direction. There is no trail at first. The larches and red vegetation here during larch season are amazing!

6. Continue down the ridge, looking to the right, where the obvious trail/road will eventually appear. Once on the trail follow it down to the top of a ski lift and then continue down using ski runs and access roads back to the parking area.

▲▲ *A staircase of beautiful rock to ascend.*

▲ *Heading down Haig Ridge. Aim for the end of the rainbow on the right side – that's where the trail is (don't count on a rainbow being there to show you the way, though!).*

17 Middlepass Lakes

A long bike and hike to three beautiful lakes under the impressive walls and slopes of Rainy Ridge and Three Lakes Ridge.

DISTANCE 20 km return
HEIGHT GAIN 800 m
HIGH POINT 2150 m
STRENUOUS length
SUMMER, EARLY FALL

Start: From Pincher Creek, drive west on Highway 507. Turn left onto Highway 774. Drive 27 km and turn right, into the

Castle Mountain ski resort. Park near the far left corner of the parking lot, where a road leads to a footbridge crossing the West Castle River.

Difficulty: Gravel roads and good trails all the way. Biking the approach is strongly recommended.

1. Cross the river on the footbridge and bike or hike 2.6 km to an important junction.

2. Take the signed right fork to Middle Kootenay Pass and continue up. Stay on your bike if you are riding. Some 3 km up, you reach an open area, where most people will leave their bikes. The trail now goes up to the right, becoming rockier and much steeper.

3. It's about a 2.3 km grind up to a high point overlooking Middle Kootenay Pass. Continue on the trail over to the other high point, where you can see the scenic valley to the southwest.

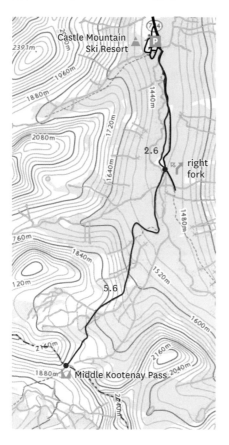

▲ After descending a short distance down the other side of Middle Kootenay Pass, Nathan McMurray turns left onto the Middlepass Lakes trail. PHOTO DAVE MCMURRAY.

▼ Nathan looks for a good fishing spot around the third lake. PHOTO DAVE MCMURRAY.

Exploring the first lake.

4. Hike down the other side of the pass for a very short distance and look for a faint trail on the left (see photo). Follow it for a short distance to another trail branching off to the left. This is the trail to the Middlepass Lakes.

5. The Middlepass Lakes Trail slide-slopes the southwest side of Rainy Ridge for about 1.7 km. Follow the trail to the first of the three lakes and then on to the second and third. All three are worthy of exploration, but the third is especially scenic and has a primitive campsite.

6. Explore the lakes as desired and then return the way you came in or do the extension to the summit of Rainy Ridge.

Going farther to the summit of Rainy Ridge

Steep scree ascent to a magnificent viewpoint. Bit of a grunt with some scrambling, but highly recommended.

DISTANCE add 2.4 km return
HEIGHT GAIN add 320 m
HIGH POINT 2469 m
STRENUOUS steepness and length

1. From the third lake, return to the lake outlet and look for a trail that starts ascending the mountain, going in a northeast direction. Follow your nose up steep terrain to a col between the Rainy Ridge summit block and its western outlier.

2. From the col simply follow the ridge eastward and southward to the summit. Again, expect steep terrain, minimal trails and some easy scrambling. Take in the splendid view and then return the same way you came in. Once you near the col, it is possible to take a more direct route to the third lake, down steep scree slopes of red argillite. If you are comfortable surfing the scree this is the way to go.

FACING PAGE FROM TOP *From the col between Rainy Ridge and its western outlier, the route up Rainy Ridge is obvious.* PHOTO DAVE MCMURRAY; *The magnificent view from Rainy Ridge.* PHOTO DAVE MCMURRAY; *Looking down the more direct descent route to the third lake.* PHOTO DAVE MCMURRAY.

CROWSNEST

Lundbreck Falls is a terrific little stop on the drive to Crowsnest Pass.

18 Hillcrest Mountain

It's not Turtle Mountain, but this mostly off-trail hike has a charm of its own and leads to a wonderful viewpoint.

DISTANCE 7 km return
HEIGHT GAIN 680 m
HIGH POINT 2185 m
STRENUOUS steepness
**LATE SPRING, SUMMER,
   EARLY FALL**

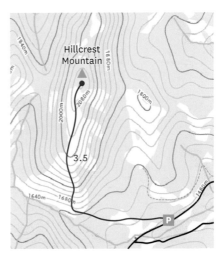

Start: Drive west on Highway 3 towards Crowsnest Pass. Turn left onto East Hillcrest Drive (1.2 km west of the Leitch Collieries). Drive 2.1 km and turn left onto Adanac Road. Drive 5.4 km to a parking area on the right side of the road.

Difficulty: Short logging road hike, followed by a steep off-trail hike up the south ridge to the summit. Some easy scrambling and route-finding near the top.

1. From the parking area hike the main trail for a few minutes, quickly intersecting another trail.

2. Turn left (west) onto that trail and hike west for about 10 minutes to the bottom of the south ridge, at approximately GR878889.

3. Leave the trail and hike up the south ridge. The bush is not terrible and disappears several hundred vertical metres up. Getting around or over deadfall will be the crux of this section, but even that is a relatively simple task. It is particularly interesting to see the old remnants and new growth on this slope, after the 2003 fire decimated the area. Note that as new growth appears this route may become more challenging.

4. A rock band is eventually reached and can be scrambled up or circumvented on either side. Above the rock band, follow the south ridge for about 1.5 km to the summit. The view of the Flathead Range, featuring Andy Good Peak, Mount Coulthard, Mount Ptolemy and Mount Darrah, is excellent.

5. Return the same way you came in. Alternate and/or more direct descent routes may look enticing, but they end up being more hassle than they are worth.

▲ *A winter view of Hillcrest Mountain from near the parking area. The ascent route goes up the left skyline.* PHOTO VERN DEWIT.

▼ *Zosia Zgolak, Ali Shariat and Asieh Ghodratabadi leave the trail to ascend the south ridge.* PHOTO SONNY BOU.

FACING PAGE FROM TOP *Naomi Kaya and Wietse Bijlsma tackle a rock band near the end of the south ridge. The band is avoidable by going around to the right side.* PHOTO VERN DEWIT; *At the end of the south ridge, it's an easy and very scenic hike to the summit.* PHOTO VERN DEWIT.

19 Poker Peak

A short but steep grind up to the terrific summit and viewpoint.

DISTANCE 1.1 km return
HEIGHT GAIN 210 m
HIGH POINT 1936 m
STRENUOUS steepness
SUMMER, EARLY FALL

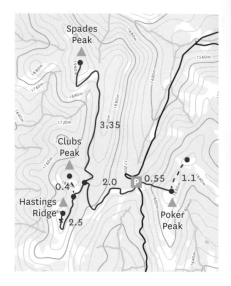

Start: Drive west on Highway 3 towards Crowsnest Pass. Turn left onto East Hillcrest Drive (1.2 km west of the Leitch Collieries). Drive 2.1 km and turn left onto Adanac Road. Drive 8.9 km to the high point of the road and park on the other side of the cattle grate.

Difficulty: Steep grassy/rocky slopes. Trail for some of the ascent, but mostly off-trail. Hiking poles are useful for this trip.

1. Staying on the right (south) side of the barbed wire fence, hike east, up the steep west face of Poker Peak directly to the summit. The hike to the top is relentlessly steep, but it's straightforward and will take 30–50 minutes for most people. Return the same way you came in.

Going farther to a minor summit to the north

Going either north or south (to Maverick Hill) along the ridge are options, but the north extension is recommended. Pleasant ridge-walking and some extra exercise.

DISTANCE add 2.2 km return
HEIGHT GAIN add 20 m
HIGH POINT 1915 m
EASY

1. Hike 1.1 km north to the next high point and then return the same way you came in. Be discerning about attempting any alternative descent routes, as new tree growth and steep terrain may make them difficult.

◄ *Three Crowsnest favourites are part of the summit view: Crowsnest Mountain (distant left), Hillcrest Mountain and Turtle Mountain.*

▲ *Looking up at the ascent slope from the parking area.*

▲ *Looking south along the ridge to Maverick Hill.*

▼ *Approaching the high point to the north. Cool snow scenery can be the reward for early-season attempts, but the area might not be accessible.*

20 Hastings Ridge South (Clubs Peak)

Easy hike to a fascinating old mine pit. Great views of the Flathead Range and much more. Note that this is not the Hastings Ridge indicated by the trail signs.

DISTANCE 7 km return

HEIGHT GAIN 200 m

HIGH POINT 1940 m

MODERATE

LATE SPRING, SUMMER, EARLY FALL

Start: Drive west on Highway 3 towards Crowsnest Pass. Turn left onto East Hillcrest Drive (1.2 km west of the Leitch Collieries). Drive 2.1 km and turn left onto Adanac Road. Drive 8.9 km to the high point of the road and park on the other side of the cattle grate.

Difficulty: Logging road hike or bike, with options for off-trail hiking and exploration.

1. The obvious logging road heads west and up. Hike or bike it for about 2 km to a signed intersection. Turn left towards Clubs Peak. Ignore the sign that says Hastings Ridge and Spades Peak.

Summit view to the west from Hastings Ridge South.

2. Shortly after, you'll come to an open area. The signed steep trail to the right goes up Clubs Peak. Stay left and hike around the summit of Hastings Ridge South to a fine viewpoint that overlooks an old mine pit.

3. It is well worth the effort to explore the pit, right in it and/or on the ridge to the west. The mining has exposed some beautiful layers of rust-coloured (oxidized) rock.

4. Either return to the viewpoint and ascend the south ridge to the summit or go around the pit on the west side and route-find your way to the top via the north side.

5. After taking in the terrific view from the summit of Hastings Ridge South, return to the open area, either the way you came in or via the north side as described below.

6. Hike down the north ridge of the peak. The terrain is steep in places and requires some off-trail travel. Intersect an obvious old logging road, turn right and make your way back to the open area in short order.

See page 94 for map.

First view of the abandoned open mine pit.

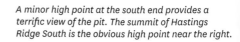

A minor high point at the south end provides a terrific view of the pit. The summit of Hastings Ridge South is the obvious high point near the right.

Going farther to Clubs Peak

Steep but very short hike to a nice summit.

DISTANCE	add 800 m return
HEIGHT GAIN	add 80 m
HIGH POINT	1950 m
STRENUOUS	steepness

Summit view from Clubs Peak. Hastings Ridge South is at the right.

Short and steep to the top.

1. Return to the open area with the trail sign for Clubs Peak and up you go. The terrain is steep throughout and gets very steep right at the end. Enjoy the view and then return the same way you came in.

21 Spades Peak

Pleasant logging road hike or bike to one of the better viewpoints in the area.

DISTANCE 11 km return
HEIGHT GAIN 300 m
HIGH POINT 2016 m
MODERATE
LATE SPRING, SUMMER, EARLY FALL

Start: Drive west on Highway 3 towards Crowsnest Pass. Turn left onto East Hillcrest Drive (1.2 km west of the Leitch Collieries). Drive 2.1 km and turn left onto Adanac Road. Drive 8.9 km to the high point of the road and park on the other side of the cattle grate.

Difficulty: Logging road hike, with options for off-trail hiking.

1. The obvious logging road heads west and up. Hike or bike it for about 2 km to a signed intersection. Turn right, towards Spades Peak and Hastings Ridge.

2. In approximately 350 m, you'll reach another intersection. Turn right, as signed.

3. Hike about 3 km to the summit. The final section involves several long switchbacks. Just before reaching the summit, a line of vibrantly coloured rock can be seen and makes for an interesting diversion. Return the same way you came in. Completing Clubs Peak and/or Hastings Ridge South is also an option.

See page 94 for map.

FACING PAGE FROM TOP *Hillcrest Mountain is the feature peak to the north; Stunning rock and sun-bleached dead trees are featured right near the summit.*

▼ *Approaching the summit block of Spades. Note the switchbacks.*

22 Frank Slide Trail

An up-close look at the incredible devastation caused by the 1903 collapse of Turtle Mountain. A must-do trip for all.

DISTANCE 1.5 km loop

HEIGHT GAIN 35 m

VERY EASY

LATE SPRING, SUMMER, FALL, BUT CAN BE ACCESSED YEAR-ROUND

Start: Drive west on Highway 3, past Bellevue, towards the town of Frank. Turn right (north) onto the Frank Slide Interpretive Centre road and continue to the parking lot.

Difficulty: Good trail with some easy rock steps to negotiate.

Brianne and Penny Hobbs, backdropped by what is left of Turtle Mountain. PHOTO MATTHEW HOBBS.

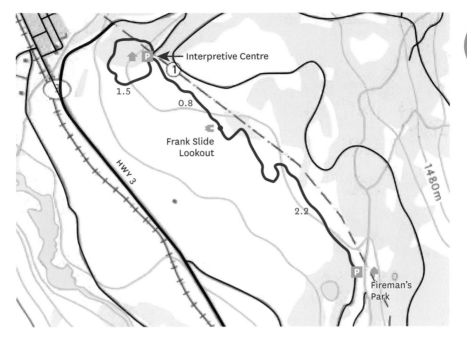

Interpretive Centre
1.5
0.8
Frank Slide
Lookout
HWY 3
2.2
1480m
Fireman's
Park

1. The trailhead is clearly marked. Follow the trail down into the debris of the slide. As you are looking at Turtle Mountain, try to envision what the mountain looked like before approximately 100 million tons of rock separated from it, burying part of the town of Frank and taking 90 human lives.

2. The trail eventually circles around the interpretive centre and then goes back up to the parking lot. Conglomerate rock and pleasant forest hiking are the highlights of the latter half. Consider a walk through the interpretive centre afterwards. There is a fee, but it's well worth it.

Gary and Karen Christison ("Papa" and "Nannie"), Mera, Penny, Crux, Matt and Brianne Hobbs enjoy the rock steps on the well-designed trail. PHOTO GORD HOBBS.

Going farther to Frank Slide Lookout and Bellevue Kiosk

Short hike to a viewpoint of the Frank Slide and then a pleasant forest walk to Bellevue if you want some extra exercise.

> DISTANCE add 1.7–6 km return (note: for a one-way trip (3 km), leave a car at Fireman's Park in Bellevue}
>
> HEIGHT GAIN add 20–150 m
>
> EASY

1. From the trailhead (the same one as for Frank Slide) hike up some rocky steps and then follow the trail around to the right, over a wooden cattle guard, and continue for about 800 m to the signed Frank Slide Lookout. This is the best view of the slide. If satiated, return the same way you came in.

2. To continue, keep following the trail as it moves away from the slide. The trail then descends to a creek, which is crossed on a small wooden bridge.

3. After crossing the creek, stay on the trail, now curving around to the left. When you see another trail branching off to the right and uphill, take that one. This trail eventually takes you to a three-way signed

Pat Hobbs (Grandma) leads Mera Hobbs through the forest walk that goes back up to the interpretive centre. PHOTO MATTHEW HOBBS.

intersection. Take the fork going slightly down towards the Bellevue kiosk.

4. It's up to you how far you go from here. If you have a second vehicle waiting at Fireman's Park in Bellevue (see 5 just next for driving directions), follow the trail signs to that location. If not, hike as far as you want to go and then return the same way you came in. There is a good view of Turtle Mountain and Bluff Mountain from a hill to the right, as you near the end of the trail.

5. Driving directions for Fireman's Park in Bellevue: from Frank Slide head east on Highway 3 and turn left onto the West Bellevue access road (21 Ave). Turn left onto 208 St Turn left onto 25 Ave and follow it to the parking lot.

FACING PAGE FROM TOP Approaching the wooden cattle guard, only minutes from the start; View from Frank Slide Lookout. For those going to the end of the Bellevue Kiosk trail and returning the same way, there is a good view of the slide from a nearby hill.

23 Livingstone Ridge (South Peak)

An advanced hike/scramble for those looking for a challenge. Varied terrain and outstanding scenery and views make this one a personal favourite.

DISTANCE 13 km return
HEIGHT GAIN 900 m
HIGH POINT 2295 m
STRENUOUS steepness and length
SUMMER, EARLY FALL

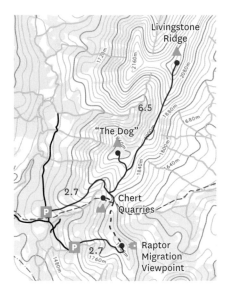

Start: Drive west on Highway 3, past Bellevue, and take the turnoff to the Frank Slide Interpretive Centre. After 1.1 km, turn onto the gravel road on the left. Go 1.5 km along the gravel road and turn left. Drive 100 m and park off to the side, at the obvious old road/cutline.

Difficulty: Rocky terrain and steep, off-trail travel, with some route-finding and mild exposure.

1. Hike 2.1 km up the old road to the point near the ridge. Note that about three-quarters of the way up, the road actually takes a sharp left turn when it appears to go straight, up a very steep slope.

2. Nearing the ridge, look left for a faint but obvious trail going up. The trail soon disappears but as long as you are going up and generally to the right the route is obvious. Note the nearby high point to the left. It is called "The Dog" and makes a good consolation objective if Livingstone Ridge feels to be too much (see #24 Livingstone Chert Quarries for a description).

3. A detailed route description from here is unnecessary. Simply follow your nose to the summit. The journey there is very

interesting, with varied terrain, some minor route-finding, and mild exposure for one short section. Expect to have to back up for short distances to find easy routes down a few rock bands. Staying on the ridge throughout gives the most enjoyable experience, but bypassing sections on the right side is possible in most cases.

4. Enjoy a spectacular summit view and then return the same way you came in.

FACING PAGE FROM TOP The trail to the left that branches off the road near the ridge. The route goes up and to the right eventually; Approaching the narrow section along the ridge. The summit is the obvious high point at the right; Typical terrain on the ridge. If this looks scary, this trip may not be for you.

24 Livingstone Chert Quarries ("The Dog")

The highlights of this trip are the views along the way, not the chert quarries.

DISTANCE 5.4 km return

HEIGHT GAIN 360 m

HIGH POINT 1850

MODERATE

LATE SPRING, SUMMER, EARLY FALL

Start: Drive west on Highway 3, past Belle-vue, and take the turnoff to the Frank Slide Interpretive Centre. At 1.1 km, turn onto a gravel road on the left. Go along the gravel road for 1.5 km and turn left. Drive 100 m and park off to the side, at the obvious old road/cutline.

After about 1.5 km the trail swings around to the right.

Difficulty: Good trail all the way. Steep in places.

1. Hike about 2.2 km up the old road to the ridge. Note that about three-quarters of the way up, the actual road takes a sharp left turn when it appears to go straight, up a very steep slope.

2. From the ridge turn right and hike up to the base of the powerline tower.

3. The inconspicuous remains of the quarries, now overgrown with vegetation and containing very little chert, sit about 100 m south of the tower (hike towards Turtle Mountain). Chert is a hard, fine-grained rock that Indigenous people used for making tools and flints. You may be under-whelmed by the quarries themselves, but

▲ At the base of the powerline towers. The
quarries are to the right from this vantage point.

▼ A small piece of chert at the upper right.

there are plenty of other sights to behold. Return the same way you came in. Other options here include Livingstone Raptor Viewpoint, "The Dog" or Livingstone Ridge.

See page 106 for map.

Going farther to "The Dog"

An excellent viewpoint that requires not too much nor too little effort to reach.

DISTANCE add 3.6 km return

HEIGHT GAIN add 225 m

HIGH POINT 2025 m

STRENUOUS steepness

1. Return to the ridge and look for a faint trail just below the ridge heading up in a northerly direction (see photo for Livingstone Ridge). "The Dog" is the nearly high point to the left of the trail.

2. Follow the trail upward. It becomes fainter but the route is obvious. As you gain elevation note the forest between the summit and the ridge. The goal is to bypass this forest by cutting to the left on open slopes before reaching it. Then ascend steep, grassy slopes to the top. There are two summit cairns: one at the highest point and one a short distance down the ridge to the southwest. Both are worthy of a visit. Return the same way you came in.

A good place to leave the ridge and cut across the slopes, below the trees.

*Summit view north, towards Livingstone Ridge
South (right) and Morin Peak (left)*

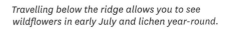

*Travelling below the ridge allows you to see
wildflowers in early July and lichen year-round.*

25 Livingstone Raptor Migration Viewpoint — Piitaistakis

Steep and interesting hike to a fantastic viewpoint, world-famous for birdwatching in spring and fall.

DISTANCE 5.4 km return

HEIGHT GAIN 350 m

HIGH POINT 1925 m

MODERATE

LATE SPRING, SUMMER, FALL

Start: Drive west on Highway 3, past Bellevue, and take the turnoff to the Frank Slide Interpretive Centre. Drive 1.1 km and turn onto the gravel road on the left. Drive the gravel road for 3 km to an open meadow. The road gets quite rough and may be impassable at the 2.5 km mark — park there if that's the case and walk up the road to the meadow.

Difficulty: Good to faint trail for most of the ascent. Some easy boulder hopping to get to the top.

1. Pick up an obvious double-track trail as it leaves the meadow, heading upward. The trail soon becomes a single track and gets steeper. Higher up, sections of it may be overgrown and fainter, but a noticeable trail always appears shortly after.

2. When the view to the south opens up, look for the remnants of an old building to the right. Work your way up to the old road above the building.

3. The summit is directly above the building and can be reached easily by following the old road southward at first. The road switchbacks and the route to the top becomes obvious. Route-find your way up to the high point and a great 360° panorama. Return the same way you came in or continue the trip to the chert quarries.

See page 106 for map.

The ascent starts from this meadow. Note the obvious double-track trail.

▲ *The old building. The summit is directly above this. Note the distant "Dalek" communication tower if you intend to extend the trip.*

▼ *The view towards Livingstone Ridge South is one of the summit highlights.*

Going farther to the Livingstone chert quarries

A pleasant addition to your day.

DISTANCE add 2.4 km return
HEIGHT GAIN add 50 m
HIGH POINT 1850 m
EASY

1. Hike northwest down and up to the next high point, complete with a communications tower that somewhat resembles a Dalek (for *Doctor Who* fans).

2. Turn north and hike down to the base of a powerline tower. The inconspicuous remains of the quarries, now overgrown with vegetation, sit about 100 m south of the tower (hike towards Turtle Mountain).

You may be underwhelmed, but there are plenty of other sights to behold including "The Dog," or Livingstone Ridge.

3. Return the same way you came in. To avoid gaining elevation back up to the Raptor viewpoint, follow the double track leaving the quarries, heading south. The trail quickly becomes a single track and goes around the mountain to eventually join up with your ascent route. This trail peters out occasionally, but as long as you are traversing, without gaining or losing elevation, you will find your way back.

▲ *Easy traverse over to the next high point.*

▼ *The chert quarries, with "The Dog" in the background. Highly recommended if you have the time (see #24, Livingstone Chert Quarries).*

26 Turtle Mountain (North Peak)

A must-do trip. To see the devastation from the 1903 rock slide from above is shocking.

DISTANCE 6.2 km return

HEIGHT GAIN 780 m

HIGH POINT 2110 m

STRENUOUS steepness

LATE SPRING, SUMMER, EARLY FALL

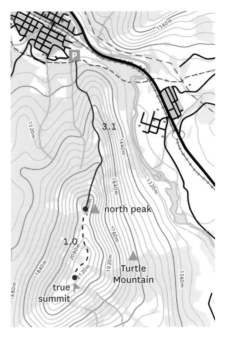

Start: Drive west on Highway 3, past the town of Frank, and turn left at the "Blairmore Centre access" sign. Follow the signs to "Turtle Mountain Trail."

Difficulty: Trail all the way to the north peak, but some steep sections with loose rock.

1. From the parking area hike down into the dip and find the obvious trail on the other side (marked with rock painted yellow as of 2018).

2. The trail is steepest near the beginning and can be tricky and very slippery when wet. Follow it carefully, making your way to the north ridge of the mountain.

3. Once on the ridge it's a simple matter of following the trail all the way up to the north peak. Although the trail lies west of the ridge, there are several sections where it is fun to travel right alongside the increasingly precipitous ridge. The rock is solid and the views are terrific. From the north peak, take in the jaw-dropping view that separates the north peak from the true summit, and then return the same way you came in or consider the difficult traverse to the south peak.

▲ *The start of the trip: down the hill and find the trail on the right.* PHOTO PARVEEN BOORA.

▼ *Typical terrain on the awesome north ridge of Turtle.* PHOTO PARVEEN BOORA.

Summit view of the devastation from the north peak. PHOTO PARVEEN BOORA.

Going farther to the true summit

A very challenging hike/moderate scramble that takes you right into the heart of the destruction and up to the highest point of the mountain.

DISTANCE	add 2 km return
HEIGHT GAIN	add 250 m
HIGH POINT	2210 m
STRENUOUS	steepness

1. Downclimb tricky terrain into a maze of deep fissures. There are many trails and routes through this section. The easiest route stays well to the right (west) of the ridge. Be very careful if you decide to explore the fissures.

2. Climb up the other side. Again, there are plenty of route options, from very steep hiking to moderate scrambling.

3. Persist over a couple of false summits to the true summit, where you can take a lunch break on the helipad. Return the same way you came in.

Looking over to the true summit and the interesting terrain to get there. PHOTO PARVEEN BOORA.

117

FROM TOP The author and his sister-in-law checking out some of the fantastic fissures and rock formations. PHOTO MARK NUGARA; Pleasant ridge hiking, but go slow. Lots of loose rubble and potential exposure; View to the south during a rare inversion.

27 Saskatoon Mountain

For those who don't mind some steep off-trail travel, a fine viewpoint of much of the Crowsnest area.

DISTANCE 4.4 km return

HEIGHT GAIN 270 m

HIGH POINT 1820 m

MODERATE

SUMMER, EARLY FALL

Start: Drive west on Highway 3 to Coleman and turn right (north) on Highway 940 (40) — Forestry Trunk Road. Drive 3.9 km to a cattle grate and park immediately on the other side.

Difficulty: Good trail to get to the base of the mountain, then faint animal trails and sometimes no trail for the remainder. Note that this is the shortest route to the summit with the least amount of elevation again and not the route that starts with the Miner's Path hike, #28.

1. Hike the obvious trail heading west towards the objective.

Crowsnest Mountain is always eye-catching.

2. Eventually the trail veers left. Keep going straight, following other trails, basically straight up the mountain.

3. Approaching the ridge, veer right, eventually intersecting the south ridge trail, and follow the ridge to the summit. This requires a small elevation loss before reaching the relatively open summit. Enjoy the view of Crowsnest Mountain and others and then return the same way you came in.

▲ *View of the route up from near the parking area. The ascent is more interesting than it looks!*

▼ *Turtle Mountain is also recognizable from the summit.*

28 Miner's Path

Pleasant, easy and satisfying hike alongside Nez Percé Creek to a waterfall and a few old mining artifacts.

DISTANCE 2 km return

HEIGHT GAIN 100 m

VERY EASY

YEAR-ROUND; LATE SPRING IS RECOMMENDED BECAUSE WATER LEVELS ARE HIGHER THEN

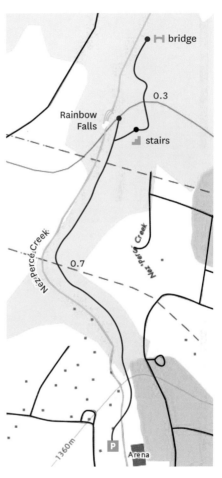

Start: Drive west on Highway 3 to the west end of Coleman and follow the signs for Miner's Path as follows. Turn right onto 76 St, take another immediate right and then a quick left into the parking area.

Difficulty: Good trail throughout.

1. Hike the obvious path alongside the creek. Ignore the second bridge that goes to the west side of the creek. It's 700 m to Rainbow Falls and a well-designed area to enjoy the water scenery.

2. Ascend the wooden stairs to get above the creek and continue going northward for about 50 m.

3. Turn left onto another trail and follow it for about 120 m to a bridge and a flume coming down from the right. The bridge is the end of the line for this trip, but there is the option to continue on trails going farther north. They offer some additional exercise, but not much in terms of scenery. Return the same way you came in.

▲ *Rainbow Falls.*

▼ *The bridge and flume at the end of the trip.*

29 Ironstone Lookout (Willoughby Ridge)

Straightforward hike up an access road to a lookout and a terrific viewpoint.

DISTANCE 14 km return

HEIGHT GAIN 550 m

HIGH POINT 2070 m

MODERATE

SUMMER, EARLY FALL

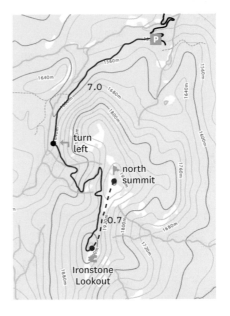

Start: Drive west on Highway 3 into Coleman. Turn left at the "York Creek staging area" sign (86 St) and follow the signs to the corner of 81 St and 13 Ave. Zero your odometer here. Continue on the gravel road for 2 km to the York Creek staging area. Drive the now rougher road for about 2.3 km to a bridge over North York Creek. After crossing the bridge, continue for 1.2 km and park off to the right where a narrower ATV trail continues going straight and the main road veers sharply to the left.

Difficulty: Good ATV trail/road throughout.

1. Hike or bike the road for 2 km to an intersection. Take the left fork. Hike another 900 m to another intersection and again take the left fork.

2. The left fork goes steeply uphill. This is the Ironstone Lookout trail. Follow it easily for 4.1 km all the way to the lookout. If the lookout is staffed, be respectful, considerate and polite to the occupants. Return the same way you came in.

3. Optional. If you are craving a little more exercise, the slightly lower high point to the north is about 700 m away and easy to reach. Return to the lookout before making your descent off the mountain — shortcutting down to the trail will be self-defeating.

THIS PAGE FROM TOP *Dinah Kruze takes the second left fork that is the start of the lookout road.* PHOTO BOB SPIRKO; *Views of the Flathead Range are spectacular already and you're only halfway up.*

FACING PAGE FROM TOP *Last few steps to Ironstone Lookout; Sonny Bou and Bob Spirko look back at the true summit from the north summit.* PHOTO DINAH KRUZE.

30 North York Creek

Unique hike/bike to the remains of a plane that crashed in the valley in 1946.

DISTANCE 16 km return

HEIGHT GAIN 480 m

HIGH POINT 1965 m

STRENUOUS length

SUMMER, EARLY FALL

Start: Drive west on Highway 3 into Coleman. Turn left at the "York Creek staging area" sign (86 St) and follow the signs to the corner of 81 St and 13 Ave. Zero your odometer here. Continue on the gravel road for 2 km to the York Creek staging area. Drive the now rougher road for 1.9 km and park off to the left side at a pullout. The trailhead is a few hundred metres farther down the road, but there is a "no parking" sign there.

Difficulty: Good trail throughout, with a few steep rocky sections. Biking some or most of it is possible.

1. Hike down the road to where a bridge goes over North York Creek. Do not cross the bridge, though. Instead, start hiking or biking the marked ATV/hiking trail ("111").

2. The trail crosses North York Creek twice. Ignore a prominent trail branching off to the left after the first crossing.

3. Eventually this trail intersects with the other approach trail at a bridge. Here you will also see the first sign for the "Plane Crash." Stay right and follow the trail all the way to the crash site. The remains of the wreckage are in trees and scattered around the area. Above the site sits an open area to take a break and enjoy the surroundings. Return the same way you came in.

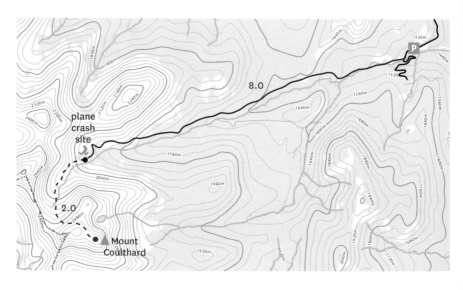

▲ Bob Spirko hikes the upper reaches of the trail. PHOTO DINAH KRUZE.

▼ The plane crash site is a little higher up and to the left. PHOTO VERN DEWIT.

Going farther to the summit of Mount Coulthard

A long and very steep hike/scramble to an outstanding viewpoint.

DISTANCE add 4 km return	
HEIGHT GAIN add 660 m	
HIGH POINT 2624 m	
STRENUOUS steepness and length	

1. From the open area above the crash site, follow a steep trail on the right side of the drainage up to the bowl above.

2. Hike on rubble into the bowl, until a feasible route to the left becomes obvious. The grassy slopes, when dry, are often the best option. Start up these deceivingly steep slopes to the summit ridge.

The main attraction of the wreckage

3. Coulthard has three summits, the east one being the highest. Upon reaching the ridge, find a good goat trail that bypasses the centre summit on its north side, and follow this to the summit.

4. The north summit can be reached with relative ease, but the centre summit requires route-finding and scrambling. Go for either or both if you have the time and inclination. Otherwise, return the same way you came in.

FACING PAGE FROM TOP Great rest area above the crash site. Also the starting point for the Mount Coulthard ascent. PHOTO VERN DEWIT; The main ascent slopes. The centre summit is seen here and the route to the true summit stays left (north) of that. PHOTO BOB SPIRKO; On the ridge, bypassing the north summit (centre of the photo) and heading to the true summit at the right. PHOTO VERN DEWIT.

31 Star Creek Falls

An easy hike to a good viewpoint above an impressive waterfall or an adventurous and tricky scramble right up the creek to the base of the waterfall, or both!

DISTANCE 2.4 km return

HEIGHT GAIN 45 m

EASY TO VERY CHALLENGING

LATE SPRING, SUMMER, FALL

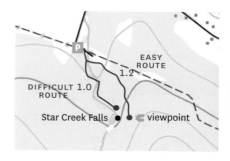

Start: Drive west on Highway 3 through Coleman and turn left at the "Coleman West Access" sign. Turn right onto 70 St, then right again onto 17 Ave. In 400 m the road veers off to the left. Turn right onto 16 Ave and drive 1.7 km to the corner of 16 Ave and 54 St. Turn left onto 54 St and either go about 100 m before parking on the side of the road or drive up the rocky hill (high-clearance vehicle is nice here), turn left at the top and drive down to Star Creek, 100 m down the hill.

Approaching Star Creek. The trail that branches off to the right just before the creek is the one you want, not the one higher up.

Difficulty: Sometimes faint but good trail for the easy route. Potentially challenging creek crossings and tricky scrambling for the difficult route.

1. If parked 100 m along 54 St, hike the remainder of the road, up a hill. Turn left at the top and hike down to Star Creek.

2. Just before reaching the creek, turn right onto the trail that parallels the west bank of the creek.

Along the easy route: Star Creek Falls from the viewpoint.

3. In short order you'll reach a bridge. For the easy route to the viewpoint go over the bridge. Do not cross for the difficult, creek route.

Easy route

1. On the other side of the bridge, follow the switchback trail up the hillside.

2. Upon intersecting another trail, turn right and follow that to the viewpoint over Star Creek Falls. Return the same way you came in. Do not try to scramble down to the base of the falls. The terrain is very steep and slippery and is far more difficult to downclimb than to upclimb.

Difficult route

(Only feasible when the water is low. Be prepared to get your feet wet.)

1. Keep following the creek on its west side.

2. Eventually a couple of creek crossings are required in order to make further progress.

3. The crux is a steep, slippery section of rock that must be ascended alongside a stretch of cascading water. Even when dry the rock is slippery and dangerous. There may be rope hanging down the rock but it should be viewed with skepticism, as animals have a habit of chewing on ropes. If at all uneasy about this tricky section, retreat immediately and remember you will probably have to come back this way.

On the difficult route: the crux. Note the rope, just visible at the left.

4. Past the crux the remainder of the hike to the base of the falls is much easier.

5. For return, either retrace your steps back down the creek or scramble up steep, slippery terrain left of the waterfall up to the trail above. This route is only for those with the appropriate footwear and scrambling abilities. At the top turn left and follow that trail back to Star Creek and the start of the hike.

32 Wedge Mountain

Short but steep ascent to an excellent view of Crowsnest Mountain and others.

DISTANCE 4.4 km return
HEIGHT GAIN 430 m
HIGH POINT 1934 m
STRENUOUS steepness
LATE SPRING, SUMMER, EARLY FALL

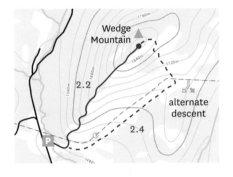

Start: Drive west on Highway 3 to the west end of Coleman. Turn right onto 61 St (signed as the "McGillivray Staging Area"). Immediately there is a somewhat convoluted intersection. Take the 23 Ave fork, going up, and drive about 2.9 km to a large open area right under the southwest ridge of Wedge Mountain. Park here and look for an obvious cutline where the powerlines are, running east–west.

Difficulty: Some off-trail travel, then trails up steep, loose terrain to gain the ridge, and easier after that. Sturdy boots required; hiking poles recommended.

1. Hike east along the wide path, across McGillivray Creek and over a cattle guard.

Niko Dewit, 9 years old at the time, powers his way up the steep lower slopes. PHOTO VERN DEWIT.

2. After the cattle guard turn sharp left, up steep slopes (no trail), trending left as you go up. The goal is to gain the south ridge.

3. As long as you are going up and left, you will eventually intercept one of several steep trails in the scree going up the south ridge. Ascend one of them, persevering up the steep, loose terrain.

4. Eventually you'll reach a small cairn and the trip gets much easier. Continue following the ridge up the mountain, sometimes on trails and sometimes without.

Self-timed photo of Niko and Dad at the summit. PHOTO VERN DEWIT.

5. A cairn and large wooden cross mark the summit (as of late 2017). To see more of the view to the north, continue north along the ridge for about 50 m. Return the same way you came in. There is an optional descent route over the north ridge and then on logging roads on the east side of the mountain for the very adventurous who are comfortable with steep off-trail travel and route-finding.

Terrific views of Crowsnest Mountain throughout. PHOTO VERN DEWIT.

33 Chinook Lake

A peaceful, leisurely and enjoyable 30- to 45-minute hike around a very pleasant lake.

DISTANCE 2 km loop

HEIGHT GAIN MINIMAL

VERY EASY

LATE SPRING, SUMMER, FALL

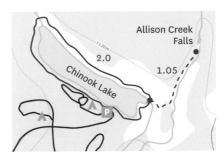

Start: Drive west on Highway 3 past Coleman. Turn right (north) onto the Allison/Chinook road and go 2.7 km. Turn left onto a gravel road and follow signs to Chinook Lake and campground. Descend a steep hill, turn a corner and park on the left.

Difficulty: Good trail all the way around the lake.

1. Go to the lake and find the trail. Hike around the lake in either direction. The south side of the lake has good views of Crowsnest Mountain and the north side of Mount Tecumseh. If you intend to also complete the Allison Creek Falls trip, the trail to the falls starts at the east end of the lake.

The north side of the lake features a good view of Mount Tecumseh.

Going farther to Allison Creek Falls

A short hike to a beautiful cascading water-fall. Washouts have made the trail more challenging. Be prepared to ford the creek if necessary.

DISTANCE add 2.1 km return from the east end of Chinook Lake

HEIGHT GAIN add 50 m

TWO TRICKY SECTIONS WHERE THE TRAIL HAS WASHED OUT; FORDING THE CREEK IS AN OPTION

1. From the east end of Crowsnest Lake by the lake outlet, instead of following the trail to the left that goes around the lake, take the wide trail to the right.

2. Hike the trail for about 300 m and look for a small track to the left going into the forest. Turn onto this.

Many people taking advantage of a beautiful, hot summer day. Crowsnest Mountain in the background.

3. Follow this trail up the west side of the creek for 750 m to Allison Creek Falls. As of June 2020 there were two sections of the trail that have been washed out. The bypass for the second washout, on the slope above the creek (see bottom photo on page 137) may feel exposed and dangerous to some. Here, there is the option to ford the creek and hike up the other side before returning to the west side. Note the water level and speed of the current before you decide to ford the creek. Spring runoff can make the creek deep and fast flowing.

4. Enjoy the cascading water and then return the same way you came in. DO NOT attempt travel farther up the creek.

▲ After turning right at the east end of Chinook Lake, hike this trail for 300 m before turning left.

▼ The second washout. The trail is on the left bank of the creek.

Allison Creek Falls.

34 Window Mountain Lake

Easy hike, with a remote feel, to a beautiful, fish-laden lake. Enjoy the serenity, or grunt your way up nearby Mount Ward, or do both.

DISTANCE 4 km return

HEIGHT GAIN 210 m

HIGH POINT 2050 m

EASY

LATE SPRING, SUMMER, EARLY FALL

Start: Drive west on Highway 3 past Coleman. Turn right (north) onto the Allison/Chinook road. Drive this rough road for about 16.8 km (only the first 2.7 km is paved) to an unsigned gravel road on the left. Either park here or turn left onto an even rougher road and drive 1.3 km to the signed trailhead.

Difficulty: Good trail to the lake. Primitive trail around the lake.

1. From the signed trailhead, start hiking up the old logging road. Do not take the narrow trail at the trailhead sign.

2. Some distance up, ignore the subsidiary road that branches off to the left. The road eventually narrows and then gains elevation up the steep headwall. Stay on the trail. There are a few rocky sections to contend with.

3. Atop the headwall, lose elevation, arriving at the lake in about five minutes. Explore the lake as desired. Circling it is highly recommended. Return the same way you came in.

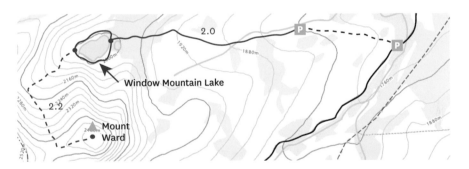

Window Mountain Lake. The route up Mount Ward starts at the back of the lake. PHOTO MATTHEW CLAY.

Going farther to the summit of Mount Ward

Awesome views but not for the faint of heart: 480 vertical metres of steep, unforgiving rubble. Hiking poles and tons of persever- ance required!

DISTANCE add 4.4 km return
HEIGHT GAIN add 480 m
HIGH POINT 2530 m
STRENUOUS steepness

1. Circle around either side of the lake (to the right is recommended) to the obvious ascent path.

This little island be can accessed by a line of carefully placed rocks.

2. A decent trail starts things off nicely, winding its way up the rubble.

3. Higher up, the summit becomes visible to the left. Stay on the grassy, vegetated terrain for as long as possible and then grind your way up the very steep rubble to a low col. Direct lines towards the summit are also possible. The view of aptly named Window Mountain is a nice surprise.

4. From the col, hike up more friendly terrain to the summit — it's farther than you think. Return the same way you came in. There is a short scree run near the col.

Looking back to Window Mountain Lake. PHOTO MATTHEW CLAY.

▲ The rubbly main ascent slopes of Ward. Summit at the left. Aim for the col to the right of the summit. PHOTO MATTHEW CLAY.

▼ That's why it's called Window Mountain Lake! The Seven Sisters and Crowsnest Mountain add to the view.

35 "Sentry Hill" and Sentry Mountain

Relatively easy and very pleasant hike to an excellent view of the west side of the Crowsnest area.

DISTANCE 6.6 km return

HEIGHT GAIN 373 m

HIGH POINT 1735 m

MODERATE one section of steep terrain

LATE SPRING, SUMMER, EARLY FALL

Start: Drive west on Highway 3 past Coleman. Turn left onto the unsigned road 1.7 km west of the turnoff to Tecumseh Road (3.2 km west of the Allison/Chinook turnoff). Turn right immediately and drive 400 m to the barbed wire gate. There is a parking spot about 100 m farther up the road or park off to the side.

After the cutline and on the second logging road. Chinook Peak is prominent throughout the trip.

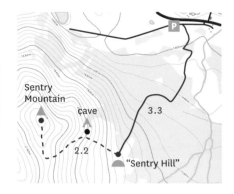

Difficulty: Logging road and a good trail most of the way.

1. Go through the barbed wire gate, remembering to close it behind you. Hike the logging road for 1.2 km, ignoring all side trails/roads.

2. Upon arriving at another barbed wire gate, turn right, onto the obvious cutline paralleling the wire fence. Hike the cutline for about 600 m.

3. At the end, turn right, onto another old logging road, again paralleling a wire fence. It's about 900 m from this point to the "Hill." The road eventually fades away, with the steepest section ahead. Don't veer off to the right at this point. Follow trails up the steep slope ahead to gentler terrain.

4. After a pleasant section of hiking through trees, the view starts to open up.

The last stretch before reaching Sentry Hill. Sentry Mountain is at the right.

Continue hiking up the trail to a minor and unofficial high point ("Sentry Hill") below Sentry Mountain. The view of the Crowsnest area from the hill is wonderful. Enjoy and then return the same way you came in or continue up to the summit of Sentry Mountain.

The view to the north includes Mount Tecumseh (left) and Crowsnest Mountain (in silhouette at the right because of the time of the day — 7:40 a.m.!)

Going farther to the summit of Sentry Mountain

Interesting ascent, fun ridgewalk and great views from a significant mountaintop.

DISTANCE add 4.4 km return
HEIGHT GAIN add 673 m
HIGH POINT 2410 m
STRENUOUS steepness and length

1. From "Sentry Hill" look for a trail that winds its way up the mountain, trending to the right. The goal is to ascend the grassy slopes to the right of the drainage. A prominent trail in the scree above, even farther right, is best avoided.

2. Once on the grassy slopes, aim for the impressive rock wall above. A good trail runs along the bottom of the rock and leads to a pleasant surprise — a cave. Getting into the cave is relatively easy but note that returning along the access trail may feel somewhat exposed to people not used to such situations. If you do decide to visit the mouth of the cave, DO NOT go any farther than the opening.

Looking up at Sentry Mountain to the right. Note the drainage just right of centre, the grassy ascent slopes to the right of the drainage, and the rock face where the cave is.

3. After your cave visit (or not), continue alongside the rock. Round a corner and then trend up and to the left alongside grassy slopes. This is the easiest and least steep route to the ridge.

4. Upon reaching the ridge, turn right (northwest) and start hiking towards the summit. There are two trails to choose from. One of them stays pretty much on the ridge throughout and would be considered easy scrambling. But if a strong west wind is blowing, I would avoid this route. The other trail stays below the ridge, on the left side. Take either to the summit. For both routes expect a few moves of easy scrambling to reach the top. Return the same way you came in. For a little variety it is possible to descend pleasant grassy slopes south of your ascent route.

FACING PAGE FROM TOP The cave. Relatively easy to hike up to but harder to get back down from; On the ridge, with Sentry Mountain dead ahead; A fantastic summit view. PHOTO VERN DEWIT.

36 Andy Good Basin (Ptolemy Creek)

Bike and/or hike into a beautiful valley lined with stunning peaks.

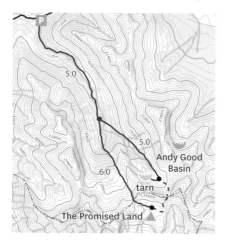

DISTANCE	20 km return
HEIGHT GAIN	780 m
HIGH POINT	2165 m
STRENUOUS	length

MIDSUMMER, EARLY FALL

Start: Drive west on Highway 3 past Coleman and Crowsnest Lake. About 1.8 km west of the end of the lake turn left onto an unsigned gravel road. Drive 3.3 km to the signed trailhead for Mount Ptolemy and Andy Good Basin.

Raff Kazmierczak negotiates one of the creek crossings.

Difficulty: Good trail throughout. Eight unbridged creek crossings. Wear runners or hip-waders (good if you are biking) for the creek crossings.

1. Hike or, recommended, bike the Ptolemy Creek trail for 5 km to a major intersection. Along the way you will have to cross the creek eight times. At approximately the 4.5 km mark take the less steep left fork, which joins up with the right shortly after.

The important intersection. Left to Andy Good Basin, right to The Promised Land.

2. From the major intersection, take the signed left fork to Andy Good Basin. The trail from here on is harder to bike but still feasible.

The shallow tarn. A more than worthwhile side trip.

The long and impressive northwest ridge of Mount Ptolemy is good company through most of the trip.

3. The trail descends to the creek. Cross the creek and then begin a long and relentless uphill grind to the end.

4. The trail simply stops around the 2165 m elevation mark. A small and shallow but very scenic tarn can be seen to the west and is definitely worth a visit. After visiting the tarn and taking in the wonderful scenery around you, either return the same way you came in or consider extending the trip as described next.

Going farther to the Andy Good Peak col

Steep ascent to the col between Andy Good Peak and an unnamed outlier. Terrific views from the col.

> **DISTANCE** add 1.6 km return
>
> **HEIGHT GAIN** add 235 m from the end of the trail
>
> **HIGH POINT** 2400 m
>
> **STRENUOUS** steepness

1. From the end of the trail, make your way up to the col between Andy Good Peak and an unnamed peak to the west (see photo). There are faint trails along the way to assist you. The easiest route involves a few easy scrambling moves and sections of steep rubble. Enjoy the view from the col and then return the same way you came. For the adventurous it is possible to traverse south over to The Promised Land and descend via that route (see the next trip for that route description in reverse).

Approaching the end of the trail. Note the col between Andy Good Peak (left) and the unnamed peak — aim for that. PHOTO RAFF KAZMIERCZAK.

Excellent view to the south from a short distance up the south ridge of Andy Good Peak. PHOTO RAFF KAZMIERCZAK.

37 The Promised Land

Venture into the wild and tortured landscape of the Andy Good Plateau, home to some of Canada's most famous caves.

> **DISTANCE** 18–22 km return
> **HEIGHT GAIN** 1000 m
> **HIGH POINT** 2470 m
> **STRENUOUS** steepness and length
> **SUMMER, FALL**

Start: Drive west on Highway 3 past Coleman and Crowsnest Lake. About 1.8 km west of the end of the lake turn left onto an unsigned gravel road. Drive 3.3 km to the signed trailhead for Mount Ptolemy and Andy Good Basin.

Difficulty: Good trail, with eight unbridged creek crossings for the approach. Steep scree up to the pass. Wear runners

Above treeline and aiming for the col (pass).

or hip-waders (good if you are biking) for the creek crossings.

2. Hike or, recommended, bike the Ptolemy Creek trail for 5 km to a major intersection. Along the way you will have to cross the creek eight times. At approximately the 4.5 km mark take the less steep left fork, which joins up with the right shortly after.

3. From the major intersection, the left fork, as signed, goes to Andy Good Basin, while the right goes to the Promised Land (see photo in the Andy Good Basin trip, #36). Take the right fork, staying on your bike if you brought one. If you intend to make a loop and return via the Andy Good Basin trail, leave your bike at the intersection.

One of the caves before reaching the pass.
PHOTO BOB SPIRKO.

4. Hike or bike the right fork for 1 km, at which point you'll reach a hiking sign and the trail narrows to a single track. Leave your bike here.

5. Follow the increasingly steep trail up the valley, past a primitive campsite, to treeline, where the route becomes more obvious. At this point you might start to see some of the caves the area is famous for. Play safe around these — many are very dangerous.

6. Continue up the valley, aiming for the col (pass) between Mount Ptolemy to the right (west) and an unnamed summit to the left (see photo on page 150). Expect to tackle loose, steep scree slopes to get to the col.

7. The barren landscape east of the col is commonly referred to as the Andy Good Plateau or The Promised Land and is home to a few of Canada's most famous caves, including Gargantua, sitting on the southwest side of the plateau.

8. Explore the plateau as much as desired. DO NOT enter any of the caves without the proper equipment and training. Return the same way you came in or make a loop and return via Andy Good Basin as described next.

See page 146 for map.

At the pass of The Promised Land. At the right is Mount Coulthard. PHOTO BOB SPIRKO.

Going farther — the loop route via Andy Good Basin

Get the most out of your day by traversing over to the Andy Good col and then descending via Ptolemy Creek.

> DISTANCE 13 km from The Promised Land back to the start
>
> HEIGHT GAIN add 150 m (add another 260 m if going to the summit of Andy Good Peak)
>
> HIGH POINT 2400 m
>
> VERY STRENUOUS steepness and length

1. Hike to the northeast side of the plateau to a point where you can see the col between Andy Good Peak and the unnamed outlier to the left of Andy Good (see top photo on page 153).

2. Turn north and hike up towards the unnamed peak, looking for an obvious and easy traverse to the col. Once you start traversing, the terrain should never be too challenging or exposed.

3. To get down to Ptolemy Creek, simply descend from the col in a northwest direction towards the trail below and to the right (see bottom photo on page 153). The descent will involve a few moves of easy scrambling but is otherwise straightforward.

4. There is a shallow tarn over to the left that is worthy of a quick side trip, if you have the time and energy. Otherwise, find the trail and follow it back to the major junction and then back to the start.

At the northeast end of the plateau. The route to the Andy Good col goes up the slope at the left and then traverses to the right, all the way to the col.

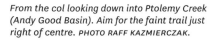

From the col looking down into Ptolemy Creek (Andy Good Basin). Aim for the faint trail just right of centre. PHOTO RAFF KAZMIERCZAK.

Contact Information

TRAVEL ALBERTA
403-627-1165

FRANK SLIDE INTERPRETIVE CENTRE
403-562-7388

Campgrounds
(see introductory information)

Emergency phone numbers

RCMP
403-562-2867

HOSPITALS
Crowsnest Pass Health Centre
403-562-5011
Cardston Health Centre
403-653-5234
Pincher Creek Health Centre
403-627-1234

EMERGENCY
911

Acknowledgements

Thank you to following for their photo contributions: Sonny Bou, Matthew Clay, Vern Dewit, Gordon Hobbs, Matthew Hobbs, Rafal Kazmierczak, Dinah Kruze, Aurore Kurc, Dave McMurray, Mark Nugara, Bob Spirko, Brad Wolcott and Raquel Wolcott. Special thanks to Shawn Benbow for his photo-editing magic. Lastly to Joey Ambrosi and Dave McMurray for sharing invaluable information and their expertise.